Excerpts from the pages of *Essays for my Father*

"In many ways, Sarah Palin's career is an amazing political story. Her catapult to the governorship of Alaska, after brief stints as a PTA president, municipal council member and mayor of Wasilla (pop. 7,028), was Frank Capra-esque. But her placement on a national ticket as the Republican vice presidential nominee is Franz Kafka-esque."

"These terrible gun massacres have brought us to an emotional cliff, more perilous than any fiscal precipice. In what has become a national nightmare, we relive the horror with 'Groundhog Day'-like repetitiveness and are left wondering if Newtown will be just one more in a growing list of killings by deranged young men armed with military-style assault weapons. Or, will the specter of 20 dead 6- and 7-year-olds, each riddled with as many as 11 bullet holes, finally overcome the powerful gun lobby's opposition to even the mildest of reforms."

"*Operation Enduring Freedom?* It is an insult to our intelligence when leaders glorify a war by affixing to it a name with such transparent intention. We're engaged in a 10-year war to prop up a corrupt government, a war in which Afghans we trained and equipped turn on and murder Americans. Enduring freedom, indeed. In Afghanistan, a land that has swallowed the armies of Alexander, Genghis Khan, Russian Tsars, the British Empire, and the Soviet Union. And, after remnants of each army leave, a land that reverts, unerringly, to its barbarous, tribal ways, its stoning of women, its repression of not only free speech, but freedom of thought, of ideas, of spirit. Just once, I'd like us to elect a president who has read a history book."

"What are we to make of our Jekyll and Hyde governor of New Jersey? Is the hard edge he often displays an essential component of leadership? In 'Lincoln,' the new Spielberg movie, we see the man revered as our greatest president acting, at times, like an overbearing, cajoling, wheeling and dealing, archetypal politician, willing to do almost anything to achieve his public policy objective. I'm not comparing Chris Christie to Lincoln, but what I am saying is that success "in the arena," as Teddy Roosevelt noted in his famous speech at the Sorbonne, sometimes requires our political leaders to be 'marred by dust and sweat and blood.' Roosevelt didn't say whose blood."

"Saddam Hussein was a bloody bastard, and we're often reminded that he killed thousands of his own people. Well, we relieved the Iraqis of that scourge, but more than 100,000 civilians are dead in the process. Are they better off as a result, or would they have been better left alone? Hussein was also a counterfoil to Iran. Yes, we took out his mythical nuclear capability, but we are now faced with a potentially real nuclear capability in Iran, unchecked by a hostile neighbor."

"The extreme right wing of the Republican Party is a bastion of Constitution worshippers, but my beef with those tri-corner-hatted, flag-waving, scripture-quoting patriots is their selective embrace of our Constitution, their hypocritical, almost slavish adherence to some of its principles while ignoring others."

"I can't remember the last time I heard a speech that didn't end in, 'God bless you and God bless the United States of America.' Frankly, I'm dismayed by the way religion now permeates our political discourse. If I could time-transport the 55 Framers from their Constitutional Convention in Philadelphia in 1787 to today's political arena, I think they'd share my consternation over what we've become, with regard not only to religious influence on politics and government but also to the complete disdain for the art of compromise."

"The 'fahgeddaboudits' and 'howyadoons' spewed forth like staccato bursts from a tommy gun in HBO's mob hit, 'The Sopranos.' Tony Soprano and his crew put New Jersey on the map, but in a way that perpetuated an unfortunate stereotype. There is a different kind of Italian-American family saga that needs to be told, the one I experienced growing up in New Jersey in the 1940s and '50s. It was less exciting—everybody worked, nobody got *whacked*—but more representative of the 17 million Americans who proudly proclaim their Italian ancestry."

"What a mess those 'nattering nabobs' of neo-conservatism got us into. Just picture where we were as a nation at the end of Clinton's second term. We had a balanced budget, no wars, and a bright financial future, with the potential payoff of our national debt within a relatively short time frame. I'm not a big Clinton fan—my kids got me his autobiography as a gift six or seven years ago, and I haven't even opened it. But you have to give the man his due."

"The New Jersey Education Association and Gov. Chris Christie are going to the mattresses. So far, both sides have displayed all the finesse and restraint one might expect from a clash between headstrong Sonny Corleone and the Five Families."

"I've been a frequent critic of the New Jersey governor, but the guy is beginning to grow on me. I'll admit that it took a while to get past his abrasive manner. When they doled out *attitude* to us Jersey natives, Chris Christie was first in line."

"As a boy in the 1940s, I remember reading an article in the *New York Daily News* about the last surviving Civil War veterans and lamenting the fact that Confederates outnumbered Union soldiers. There were five or six of the Rebels left and only one or two of the 'good guys.' In 20 years, give or take, we'll be honoring the last of the World War II vets—all of them good guys."

"In a government-sponsored, taxpayer-funded program, live syphilis and gonorrhea bacteria were transported in the late 1940s from a Staten Island, New York lab to Guatemala, where they were used to intentionally infect prisoners, prostitutes, and soldiers. The purpose? To see if penicillin would be an effective cure for those venereal diseases. In other words, the United States was using human subjects for medical experimentation without their consent or knowledge, and we were doing so at about the time we were prosecuting Nazis at Nuremberg for crimes against humanity."

"What is it with Palmetto State politicians? Is there something in the air in South Carolina? Noxious fireworks fumes that accumulate in toxic quantities and waft their way to Columbia, the state capital? Has Pedro broken loose from 'South of the Border' and become a political consultant?"

"It's the same old story. Politicians taking the easy way out so they can continue their posturing, their sloganeering, and their 15-second sound bites, with as much bluster and self-assuredness as they can muster. Just once I'd like one of them to exhibit thoughtful consideration and substance on any important issue, rather than the outright certainty and pat answers they have for everything."

ESSAYS FOR MY FATHER

A legacy of passion, politics, and patriotism
in small-town America

ESSAYS FOR MY FATHER

A legacy of passion, politics, and patriotism
in small-town America

RICHARD MUTI

ESSAYS FOR MY
FATHER

A legacy of passion, politics, and patriotism
in small-town America

Cover Design: Erika L. Block
Interior Layout and Design: Erika L. Block

PUBLISHER'S CATALOGING-IN-PUBLICATION DATA:

Muti, Richard.
Essays for my father : a legacy of passion, politics, and patriotism in small-town America / by Richard Muti. -- 1st ed. -- Ramsey, NJ : [s.n.], c2013.

p. ; cm.

ISBN: 978-0-9891482-0-7

Summary: Essays for my father is a collection of essays about Gov. Chris Christie and New Jersey politics, the national political scene, unnecessary wars and wrong-headed government, rare displays of political courage, not-so-rare displays of political cowardice, an Italian-American heritage shared by 17 million Americans, public employee unions, and other public policy issues that challenge state and federal government.

1. New Jersey--Politics and government--21st century. 2. United States--Politics and government--21st century. 3. Political oratory--21st century. 4. Public relations and politics. 5. Mass media and war. 6. Christie, Chris. 7. Political planning--21st century. 8. Citizenship--United States. I. Title. II. Legacy of passion, politics, and patriotism in small-town America.

JK1759 .M88 2013
323.6--dc23   1304

CONTENTS

Part IV – The New Colossus of Trenton
Essays about *Jersey-Style* Politics and Governor Chris Christie

PREFACE

The spot every newspaper Op-Ed writer craves is page one of the Sunday Opinion section, above the fold. I've been fortunate enough to land that choice location many times in The Record of Bergen County, New Jersey's second-largest circulating newspaper. In fact, I'm probably the most prolific freelance contributor of the past ten years for North Jersey Media Group, The Record's parent company. Not only have I published dozens of opinion pieces in The Record, but I've also written more than 100 additional articles for the Ramsey Suburban News, another NJMG subsidiary, and for that media giant's NorthJersey.com website. My weekly Suburban News column and blog were both called "In the Arena," a title borrowed, of course, from Teddy Roosevelt's famous 1910 speech at the Sorbonne.

My history as a contributor to The Record provided the impetus for this book, a collection of essays that reflect the peripatetic nature of the life I've led—ideal training for a writer, if the old saw, "Write about what you know," holds true.

I spent nine years in the military—four at the Naval Academy and five as a Navy pilot—before earning an M.B.A. from Harvard Business School and going into real estate development. Within five years of my graduation from Harvard, I enrolled in Rutgers Law School in Newark, attending four nights a week for four years, and eventually became, at 40, an assistant prosecutor in the Bergen County Prosecutor's Office. Three years later, with two kids about to enter college, I switched to private practice, but also took a part-time municipal prosecutor position in Sparta, New Jersey, where I was living at the time.

I found private practice boring. My niche was prosecuting criminal cases on the side of the good guys, and I returned to the Bergen County Prosecutor's Office as soon as the opportunity arose, in 1995, to take a senior post in that office. It was a career that would have satisfied me until I no longer had the strength to pick up a case file. But it was not to be. I was summarily fired as Deputy First Assistant Prosecutor in August 2000, after I wrote to the county governing body to protest my boss's plan to spend $7 million in public money on what I considered a boondoggle.

The firing opened new doors, although it cost me dearly both personally and financially, coming as it did ten months before I was eligible for retirement health benefits and an enhanced pension. I was 60 at the time, not an advantageous age to begin job hunting. Wallowing in doubt and self-pity for months, I decided to write about the experience. When The New York Times published my article in late 2001, I got my confidence back. That piece remains one of the best things I've written, and I reprise it in this book.

I'd had a few things published here and there and always thought I had writing talent, but to have it validated by a world-class newspaper . . . well, that was special. It launched my writing career and led to a proliferation of articles about public policy and to this, my fourth book. The firing also led to my getting involved in local politics, in my father's footsteps.

After my father's death on St. Patrick's Day, 2000, I moved back to Ramsey, New Jersey, his hometown and mine, where he had served for nine years on the borough council and for close to 30 years as tax assessor. In my grief over his passing, I had to be close to streets we'd both walked, to the people we'd both known, to the roots we shared. I live around the corner from "The House on Carol Street," where my father grew up. It was a special place—a place that you'll read about in these pages.

Essays for my Father

I don't recall my father ever saying, "I love you, Son." For that matter, I don't remember him ever hugging me, although he must have when I was a child. He was not a cold man. We Muti's are simply not given to displays of affection. When I was enrolled at the U.S. Naval Academy, there was exactly such an offense in the disciplinary code: "Public Display of Affection—No midshipman shall engage in a public display of affection while in uniform. Four demerits." I am reciting the verbiage from memory after 52 years, but that was the gist of it. I never got *fried* (read: put on report) for that particular offense, although the inch-thick regulation book offered an abundance of other violations for my superiors to pick from. No worries, though, when the family visited Midshipman 4th Class Richard Muti; the banks of the Severn River in Annapolis, like everywhere else, were a hug-free zone for us.

The relationship between my father and me wasn't as extreme as that between the Rebbe and his son in Chaim Potok's *The Chosen*. There was no deliberate regime of silence between us, to toughen me for a leadership role later in life. My father's reserve was purely the result of the way he'd grown up, thrust into the role of head of family at 15.

2

My father wouldn't be considered a great man by most people, at least not in the normal sense of that word. He made no scientific discoveries, invented nothing. He built no skyscrapers. He was not a captain of industry, nor did he achieve fame in any other field. He led no armies or navies and won no medals for bravery in battle. Beyond the life spans of those who knew him, he is not likely to be remembered.

And yet, there was something about him.

I realized this about my father early in life, by observing the way his mother and brothers and sisters treated him. There was a certain deference paid, a respect. Like survivors of a long, hard struggle looking up to the person who'd endured it with them and was responsible for leading them through it. He was the person everyone in the family went to for advice or help. At Sunday family dinners when I was a child, with all the Muti siblings and their spouses gathered around, my father always sat at the head of the table and was served first by his mother and sisters.

Because I was my father's son, I was automatically entitled to an exalted position in the family. In an old photo of my grandmother surrounded by grandchildren, I'm the one she's clutching closest. Years later, after becoming head of my own family, I'd often speak with my father's sister, Aunt Sally. She would invariably end our conversations with this plea: "Richard, you take good care of your father. He's special to us."

What was there about him? What was so special? Why did he have this effect on his family? To understand, you need to know a little of the Muti family history, what went into the shaping of Mauro Richard Muti, my father.

* * *

In late 1906, Sergio Muti, 23 years old and recently discharged from the Italian army, left his home in Molfetta on the southern Adriatic coast and headed across the boot of Italy to Naples, the major port of embarkation for Italians emigrating to America. U.S. immigration officials had a special classification, probably pejorative, for the darker, less educated, and mostly poor arrivals from the lower third of the Italian peninsula: *Italian South.* Still, in those days, America was truly the land of Emma Lazarus's famous poem. It took in all comers—even those who were poor, unskilled, and illiterate, like my grandfather Sergio—so long as they were not anarchists and were healthy and willing to work.

In that regard, Sergio's story is no different from that of millions of poverty-stricken immigrants from eastern and southern Europe, leaving homes and families and enduring hellish Atlantic crossings in the bowels of over-loaded ocean liners for a better life in the New World. Some went to Argentina and Chile, establishing large European populations in those countries. Most came to America.

The ship's manifest for the *SS Hamburg*, upon its arrival at Ellis Island on November 8, 1906, described Sergio Muti as having a dark complexion and standing five feet, two inches tall. In the column that specified how much money he had with him, someone wrote in $10, but then crossed that figure out and wrote "0". Fortunately, Sergio had an older brother, Nicolo, already established here and working as a longshoreman.

My paternal grandmother, Rosaria Potenza, was just 17 when she made the crossing in 1907. She did it on her own, except for a younger sister in tow. I still remember her story of the "tempest-tost" sea voyage they endured in steerage, Grandma's first and last encounter with a boat. In later life, an immersed ankle was the most she would venture at Coney Island or the Jersey shore, so great was her dread of the ocean. But she was fearless in every other aspect of her life.

I know nothing about how my grandparents met and were married. To my regret, I never thought of asking about that when my grandmother was alive (she died in 1970 at 80), although I saw her every day of my childhood and early adulthood, except when I was away at college or in the Navy. There are so many more questions I wished I'd asked, of her and of my father.

In 1911, Sergio and Rosaria came to Ramsey, New Jersey, where he found work as a laborer paving Franklin Turnpike, an old stagecoach route that was still a dirt road in the early 1900s. They lived for a time in a small apartment at Don Bosco, a boys' boarding school. My grandfather took care of the grounds when not working on the road gang, and my grandmother cleaned for the priests. Carmella, their first child, was born in Ramsey, but after the Franklin Turnpike job ended, Sergio was out of work and, so, moved his family to Brooklyn, where he got a job on the docks, alongside his brother.

My father, Mauro, was born in the Red Hook section of Brooklyn on January 23, 1913, but shortly after his birth, the family, at my grandmother's insistence, moved back to Ramsey. She was a country girl from Calabria and had no use for city life. Over the next 15 years, another child was added about every other year—Angie (Sally), Vince, Josie, Nick, Rosie, Tony, and Jean. Nine in all. At some point, Sergio built a gray stucco house on Carol Street. It was small and crowded, and had no indoor plumbing (that convenience was added later), but it was home. As a child, I spent many happy hours in that house on Carol Street and wrote about it in an essay that *The New York Times* published in 2002.[1]

As the oldest son, my father started working early. I have his first bank book, which he kept all those years. He opened the account with his father in 1922, when he was nine years old, and deposited into it all his earnings from an assortment of jobs—newspaper boy, grocery store delivery boy, and soda jerk in an ice cream parlor. Each calendar quarter, the bank book shows a withdrawal. My father's savings went to pay the real estate taxes on the family home.

A few weeks before my father died, when his mind was beginning to deteriorate, I tried to prod him into more lucid moments with questions about his childhood. I asked him what he remembered about his mother and father. About his father, he said just three words: "Work, work, work." About his mother, he said, "The best woman." In that house on Carol Street, there was not much verbalization of emotions. They did not feel the need to remind each other about their feelings. Love, affection, loyalty—these were taken as givens; they were expressed through actions, through the everyday struggle to survive.

In 1928, tragedy struck the family. Sergio Muti, while working at a construction site, cut himself on a rusty shovel. To save the expense of a doctor, my grandfather ignored the injury. When his body became progressively worse with stiffness and pain, he went first to one doctor, then another. Finally, the third doctor correctly diagnosed the problem—tetanus, or "lockjaw" as it was called back then. But it was too late. On June 17, 1928, Sergio Muti died. He was 44 years old and left a pregnant wife and eight other children.

Just as the Great Depression was about to start, just as millions were about to be thrown out of work, just as bread lines and Hoovervilles were about to spring up everywhere, 15-year-old Mauro Richard Muti, as the oldest son, became head of the family. He accepted that responsibility without complaint and offered to quit school, but his mother insisted he finish high school. So he did both, working mornings before school and nights after school and, of course, Saturdays and Sundays.

---

[1] I loved that essay so much I included it in my first book, *Passion, Politics, and Patriotism in Small-Town America*, (WingSpan Press, 2008) and now include it in this collection, too.

A few months after Sergio died, my father's nine-year-old brother, Nick, cut his foot. The bleeding wouldn't stop, so my father carried him about a mile to the doctor's office—the same doctor who had correctly diagnosed Sergio's illness. The doctor was still owed money, probably a small sum, for the services he'd provided to Sergio, and he wouldn't treat Nick until he was paid. My father left his brother at the office, ran back home, and, somehow, he and my grandmother scraped together the money. Nick's foot was sewn up, and my father carried him back home.

My father graduated from Ramsey High School in 1930. His framed diploma hangs on my office wall as I write this essay. Although he was intelligent and showed promise as a student, college was out of the question, given his family circumstances. In addition to required studies in English, history and math, my father mostly took courses in basic business skills. His first full-time job after graduation was working as a garbage collector. It was a disgusting job then, as I'm sure it is now. In those days, the garbage was hauled to nearby pig farms, there used to fatten the stock. My father couldn't eat pork for years after. When he told me about that experience, it was as though I'd been there, myself, breathing in the stench.

Mauro dutifully turned over pay to his mother. It wasn't much, but in those days, a few dollars could feed the family for a week. Finally, though, the job got to him, and he asked his mother if she'd mind if he quit and looked for other work. He could deal with the hard work but was embarrassed to be seen by his friends collecting garbage.

Dad got a job working for Atlantic & Pacific Tea Co. and, in a few years, became produce manager for a number of its markets. His brothers and sisters were getting older by then and were helping out with the family's needs, so he could begin to think about other things besides work.

While assigned to the Ho-Ho-Kus A&P, my father was sweeping the sidewalk one day when he spied an attractive young woman walking by. Mafalda Milano, a 17-year-old Waldwick girl, had to pass the store on her way to work. She and two sisters were domestics in the home of a wealthy Ridgewood family. I don't know if it was love at first sight, but Mauro and Mafalda began courting.

My maternal grandfather, Giuseppe, tried, in the Italian tradition, to divert my father's attention to my mother's older and still unmarried sister, Elena, but my father would have none of that. He and my mother were married in April 1939. He was 26, she was 19. Later that same year,

6

they opened the Community Lunch in Ramsey, a place that could have been the prototype for establishments on Guy Fieri's "Diners, Drive-Ins, and Dives," one of the Food Channel's most popular shows. But if it were not for my mother, Mauro would probably have kept to his $25 a week job at A&P.

My father was not a risk-taker. Years later, when I owned shares in a few standardbred horses, I'd take him to the Meadowlands or Yonkers to see them race. He was financially comfortable by then, though never rich. Even when he "heard it straight from the horse's mouth" that one of my horses was ready to win, he'd make just a $2 bet, usually for place or show. And he was just as happy cashing those tickets as I was, collecting my considerably larger winnings.

My mother was the gambler—she taught me how to play poker before I was out of grammar school—and it was she who persuaded my father to open up the restaurant. As the third oldest daughter in her own large, Italian immigrant family, she'd learned to cook at her mother Pia's side and had no doubt she could manage any culinary challenge that a small luncheonette could offer. They rented a storefront on Main Street for $60 a month and bought equipment they needed with no money down from a restaurant supply house in Paterson. The economy was expanding in the run-up to the war, so suppliers were eager to take on new customers and build their businesses.

Together, "Muffie" and "Dick," as they were known, ran the Community Lunch for 16 years, staying open 24 hours a day during the war to accommodate the heavy traffic of truckers passing through town. Just about every one of their younger siblings worked in the place over the years, almost as though it were a rite of passage. I got into the act when I was tall enough to see over the top of the lunchroom counter—probably in fourth or fifth grade. My father would triple fold a white apron, just like his, and tie it around, up under my arms. I'd help out after school and on Saturdays, sweeping up, clearing tables, and washing dishes by hand (the place never had an automatic dishwasher). As I got older, I progressed to waiting on customers, working the soda fountain, and short-order cooking, besides doing the other stuff.

My father was a volunteer fireman, and he'd often run out to answer a call—his fire truck was garaged half a block away—leaving my mother alone to take care of the lunchroom. The customers, mostly townsfolk, would cooperate on such occasions, helping themselves to coffee and pie and leaving their money on the counter. One of my biggest thrills was the first time my father responded to a fire call and left me, no older than 12 or 13, in charge. My mother was probably off taking care of my younger sisters. I'll admit to being a little scared, but I managed just fine, with no serious mishaps that I can remember.

On good days at the Community Lunch, my father would count up $60 or $70 in the till at closing time. Not bad when coffee was a nickel and the blue-plate special, a dollar and a quarter. If I'd been working and was with him when he locked up, I'd get a dollar if business was good, nothing otherwise.

My parents had a dream of one day opening an Italian restaurant in Ramsey—a more formal, sit-down place and not a luncheonette, a place where my mother's cooking talents would be put to better use. They achieved their dream in 1956 with the opening of Milano Restaurant, named for my mother's family.

In the one-year interim between the closing of Community Lunch and opening of the new restaurant, I put my soda fountain skills to the test as a counterman at the new Howard Johnson's on the highway, for the huge wage of a dollar an hour. My father had taught me well: I was a star in the 28-flavor world at HoJo's and stayed an employee there through high school, even after Milano Restaurant opened.

As a lifelong resident of Ramsey and local businessman, my father knew everyone in town, not a bad springboard into politics. He belonged to the local chamber of commerce and rose to become its president. He also joined the Ramsey Republican Club and would eventually become its president, too, but not before showing a streak of independence that angered party stalwarts.

In the 1953 New Jersey gubernatorial election, my father backed maverick Republican Malcolm Forbes for the party's nomination. Forbes lost the primary to the organization's candidate, a man named Troast, and my father ended up voting for the eventual Democratic winner, Robert Meyner.

The Forbes-Troast contest was my first taste of politics. I was a seventh grader at the time and remember debating a classmate as to who was the better man to represent the party. Naturally, I took my father's side. Soon after, my father began running for local office, losing his first couple of races, for county committeeman and council—once by seven votes. I passed out leaflets with him at the train station, catching commuters as they left in the morning for jobs in New York City and as they returned home in the evening.[2] Dad finally won a seat on the Ramsey Borough Council in the mid-1950s and would never lose another election. He served nine years, five as council president, leaving office only to run for tax assessor, a full-time, paid position that was an elective office in those days, but is an appointed post now. By then, Milano Restaurant had been sold.

The business had done well, but after running through a succession of partners, including my father's brother Nick, my parents were ready to move on. The site has been home to a number of restaurants since then, the latest being the highly successful Greek seafood restaurant, Varka.

Unlike his three brothers, my father never served in the military during World War II. I don't know why and never asked him about it, but I sense it was that same feeling of obligation to look after his mother and extended family that kept him home. The draft didn't reach his age level and dependent status (he had two children by 1943) until late in the war, which ended soon after he got his 1A classification and notice to report for a pre-induction physical. Two of my uncles—Vince as a B-24 tail gunner and Tony as an infantryman in Patton's Third Army—saw combat. Vince was seriously wounded by shrapnel after more than 20 missions over France and Germany, but recovered and returned, with a Purple Heart and multiple air medals, to his pre-war job with the post office. Tony suffered no wounds and came home with his share of French and American decorations. Nick served in the Navy, but not in a war zone.

In my youth, I think I was a little ashamed of my father's failure to volunteer during the war—foolishly so, now that I look back on it. That feeling was probably a major factor in influencing me to spend a good part of my life in the military, first at the Naval Academy and then as a Navy pilot.[3]

---

[2] Fifty years later, I would pass out leaflets at that same train station, this time for my own campaign for mayor of Ramsey. Imbued with the same independent streak as my father, I ran as a Democrat—party label never meant much to me—and defeated a four-term, organization Republican in a landslide, thanks, in part, to name recognition and folks who remembered my father. The only downside to that red-letter day was that he wasn't there to see it.

[3] I never saw combat, although the Vietnam War was raging during my service, and never volunteered to go, a request the Navy surely would have granted. In a way, I'm disappointed in myself for not taking that route. We all have regrets and curiosity about "the road not taken." I've learned to live with mine.

Dad was the thriftier of my parents, by far, and we liked to poke fun at his tendency to be tight with a buck. When I delivered his eulogy in March 2000, I started out, only half-jokingly, with the assertion that almost everyone who heard the news of my father's death was saddened by it. "Almost everyone," I said, "because one group did have mixed emotions—the boys down at Midas Muffler."

My father was proud of the fact that he'd used his Midas Muffler lifetime guarantee five times on his 1983 Volvo wagon. He kept the guarantee in a strongbox, next to his will, deeds, and other important papers. In a sense, he never was able to escape the Great Depression mentality. He thought of money in terms of 1935 dollars; he loved a bargain and hated waste. Until his illness, he ate every speck of food my mother put before him, unfailingly. My mother attributed it to her good cooking, but I suspect there was a trace of remembered days when there wasn't enough.

Perhaps we need to rethink how we measure greatness. Perhaps the courage of a teenage boy, striving to hold his family together and to lift them up in the face of unimaginable hardship, is as important as courage on a battlefield. Perhaps the willingness of a young man to work relentlessly for the improvement of his and his family's status in life, to build a foundation upon which his children could reach even higher goals, counts as much as any engineering feat.

Mauro Richard Muti was human; he had his share of human frailties and shortcomings. But, in a way, my father was great, too. This book and collection of essays are dedicated to him on the 100th anniversary of his birth, January 23, 2013.

Part I
Our Country, Right or Wrong

Essays about National Issues

Not That There Is Anything Wrong with Wiccans and Druids

What Is It with Palmetto State Politicians?

Rush Limbaugh's Heart of Darkness

Chapter 1

This article first appeared in The Record, on Sunday, April 6, 2009, in the featured position on the front page of the Opinion section, along with a wonderful accompanying illustration. It is among my favorite pieces, not only because of the ongoing controversy about illegal immigration but also because of how much the heroine of the story reminded me of my own grandmother—a legal immigrant, thanks to the fortuitous time of her entry into this country, a time when the poor were grudgingly accepted.

An Immigrant's Tale

The *New* New Colossus:
"Huddled Masses" and "Wretched Refuse" Need Not Apply

Pilar Costurera's eyes are her most striking feature, as she sits across the kitchen table from me in her English as a Second Language teacher's apartment. I wanted to interview an illegal immigrant, to put a human face on what most Americans know only in the abstract. A friend helped arrange the meeting with Pilar (a pseudonym).

Her English is good, but if I lose a word or two in her accent, I need only concentrate on the eyes to fully comprehend. She is neatly dressed, and her hair looks professionally cut, giving her round face an attractive if matronly appearance. Pilar, 44, is telling me about her entries into this county and the undocumented life she has led, first in New York City, then in Bergen County, New Jersey.

The United States of America once prided itself on being a nation of immigrants, a country embracing the sentiment of Emma Lazarus's famous poem. More recently, *illegal* immigration has become an issue in presidential politics, only slightly less emotional than the Iraq war and stagnant economy. Sen. John McCain co-sponsored legislation in 2005 offering a "pathway to citizenship" for 12-14 million illegal immigrants already in this country. When polls showed a majority of Americans opposed to such leniency, McCain backpedaled.[4]

---

[4] When Sen. McCain was up for re-election in 2010, he took a harsher tone on illegal immigration, both to pacify his Arizona constituents and to beat back a primary challenge from the extreme right of his party. More recently, McCain has joined senators of both parties to propose a more reasonable solution, including a pathway to citizenship for those already here.

I ask Pilar why she didn't try to enter the United States legally. She scoffs at the idea, barely able to conceal her amusement at my naïveté. U.S. Embassy staff always deny visas to people like her, she says, and, indeed, a Hackensack, New Jersey immigration lawyer confirmed her skepticism.

"People who cross the border illegally," said attorney Melvin Solomon, "do so because they have no hope of getting here any other way. When they enter the country without a visa, they can't get legal status because they haven't been inspected by an immigration official. Unless they have a qualifying relative—a U.S. citizen with a close blood relationship—to sponsor them or a job skill in demand," Solomon added, "they don't have a prayer of getting in."

Pilar Costurera was living in Mexico City in 1995, working two jobs as a seamstress to support three children. Her husband had been murdered three years earlier, but all she says about that is "he was in the wrong place at the wrong time." Long work hours left no time for family, so Pilar resolved to go to New York City, make the big money others boasted about, and return to Mexico to be with her children.

She traveled to Nogales in the Mexican State of Sonora, across from Arizona. There, she paid $1,000 to those who would guide her through the "frontier," as she calls the border. The guides are necessary, she says, because the frontier is dangerous, with bandits on both sides.

Pilar struggles for the right English words to describe the 12-foot wall she scaled in her first border crossing, or the tunnel she belly-crawled in another, fighting claustrophobia and sending roaches and spiders scurrying, or the desert she wandered for days without food or water in yet a third crossing, or the working conditions she endured once here.

She had expected earnings of $7.80 an hour in New York—good pay when converted to *pesos*—but the reality was different. Working in a Fashion District sweatshop, she was paid piece rate—a set amount for each garment—netting her less than minimum wage. Undocumented, she could do no better.

By 2002, Pilar could bear family separation no longer. She returned to Mexico, not to stay but to lead her children back across the border, in what would become the horrific tunnel crossing. Just as they emerged on the US side, the border patrol pounced. They were captured and escorted back to Mexico.

As the family waited in Nogales, Pilar noticed Mexican children in uniforms crossing the border without hindrance to attend a Catholic parochial school in Arizona. She bought identical uniforms for her children and sent them across with the others, while she remained behind. Her children would be cared for until she could cross again. It took thirty days for her chance, but she finally made it.

As I listen to Pilar, I cannot help comparing her to my own grandmother, although my grandmother's skin was darker. At 17, Rosaria Potenza, all 4 feet, 11 inches of her, left her home in the impoverished region of Calabria in southern Italy to find a new life in America. She entered legally, at a time when immigrants were needed for menial work. Once here, she met and married Sergio Muti, an unskilled laborer from Molfetta in Puglia. They moved to Ramsey, New Jersey, in 1911, where Sergio got work paving Franklin Turnpike, a dirt road back then.

My grandparents, both illiterate and speaking little English, raised nine children in Ramsey. They would have had more, but my grandfather cut himself on a rusty shovel while digging out man-made Crestwood Lake in Allendale. He delayed getting medical attention—doctors were a luxury—and died from tetanus at 44, just as the Great Depression was about to begin. There was no workers' compensation then, no social security or health care systems, no pensions for widows of ditch-diggers.

With resourcefulness, cunning and courage, my giant of a grandmother kept her family together, reasonably fed and clothed, through the worst economic upheaval this country has known. Then, she sent three sons off to war, where they earned the Purple Heart, Air Medals and a Bronze Star, among other military honors. One son became president of the Ramsey Borough Council. One grandson became a teacher; another became a Ramsey police officer; and another became a Navy pilot and, later, mayor of Ramsey. A great-grandson served as a naval officer in the Persian Gulf War, and another great-grandson is presently serving his country in Iraq.

I see that same resourcefulness and courage in Pilar. She has five children now; two were born here and are American citizens. Taxpayers foot the bill for the children's education and medical care, although private organizations help, too. Their mother scaled a 12-foot wall, crawled on her belly through 300 feet of tunnel with three children in tow, and braved a desert to get here. Given time, who knows what heights the children of Pilar Costurera may reach, or what great deeds they may perform for their new country America, land of opportunity, nation of immigrants.

Chapter 2

When I learned of the extraordinarily high rate of suicide among returning veterans of the Iraq and Afghan wars, I wrote this piece, which appeared, fittingly, in The Record's Sunday Opinion section on Independence Day, July 4, 2010.

Our Nation's Military Under Stress

The time has come for compulsory national service for all young Americans, men *and* women.

Yes, I mean reinstating the draft, but also providing non-military alternatives for "draftees" to fulfill a required 2-year period of national service—duty assignments like becoming a teaching assistant in failed school districts, or cleaning oil spills that endanger fragile wetlands, or surveilling our borders to help control illegal immigration, or manning a much needed cyberspace defense force.

Perhaps now, during this 4th of July weekend when patriotism is at its peak, we should rethink what each of us owes our country in terms of personal sacrifice. Universal national service—with no weaseling out by the rich or politically connected—would be *payback* of the highest sort.

This is not a new idea. It's been bandied about for years, ever since the Vietnam War-era draft ended in 1973. Even with options on how to perform compulsory national service, it would likely be as unpopular today as it was 40 years ago, especially if women were required to participate. The truth, though, is that women are as capable of serving as men.

The bravery and versatility of women in our armed forces has never been more in evidence. Any erstwhile military "glass ceiling" has been blown to smithereens. Eleven percent of forces deployed to Iraq and Afghanistan since those wars began have been women; more than 100 female soldiers and marines have been killed, with scores more wounded. Women have infiltrated most of the elite military units, including ten female graduates of the U.S. Naval Academy who were assigned this year to submarine duty, one of the last all-male bastions in our armed forces.[5]

---

[5] In 2013, Secretary of Defense Leon Panetta, presumably on orders from the president, took an unprecedented step in our history and ordered military commanders to permit women to serve in combat billets, alongside males.

No one can question the ability of women, but *requiring* women to serve may be a different story. They have never been subject to the draft.

Serving in the military is no longer an important rite of passage for young men—not for today's generation and not for their parents' generation of the late 1960's and early 1970's, a time when avoiding military duty was an accepted and even admired bit of unpatriotic gamesmanship for most 20-somethings.

"The draft would be political poison," said Dr. Peter Woolley, political science professor at Fairleigh Dickinson University and director of FDU's highly regarded *PublicMind* poll. It may even be unpopular within the military. "Military leaders want to lead people who want to be led," Dr. Woolley added. "An all-volunteer force of soldiers, who are fed, housed, and re-supplied by private contractors, has given the executive branch a great deal more latitude in its military interventions than it ever had."

The urgency now is that the world has become increasingly more dangerous. America needs the resources—a larger trained military and a pool of individuals capable of helping in other ways—to deal with the new challenges it faces. Young people would themselves gain immeasurably from this service, in terms of character and leadership development, work and life experience, learned discipline, and a sense of accomplishment they will carry for the rest of their lives. It will take them time to appreciate those benefits, but when most are without meaningful work, they'd have a paying job, at least for a couple of years, excellent health and dental care, and a purpose to their lives.

Fighting two wars simultaneously has put our all-volunteer military under tremendous strain, not only because of multiple deployments to the war zones, with too little time spent at home with families, but also because of the extraordinary nature of these particular wars. Every Iraqi or Afghan civilian, no matter his or her age or sex, is a potential *smart bomb*, ready to take out an entire squad of soldiers; any roadside pile of debris could be hiding an I.E.D., for "improvised explosive device," the homemade booby traps that make every patrol on every street, alley, and goat path a survival crapshoot.

Because of such stress, compounded by three and four lengthy tours of duty in combat zones, suicide has become the second most lethal threat for men and women serving in our armed forces; but military brass have been slow to recognize the problem or find ways to deal with it.

According to a recent UPI report, 301 armed forces personnel took their own lives in 2009—the highest number since record-keeping began in 1980, surpassing the old mark of 235 in 2008. In an interview with *Time* magazine's Joe Klein, Army Chief of Staff Gen. George Casey admitted he had no idea why suicide numbers were climbing at such an alarming rate.

Members of Congress see how military suicides are affecting families in their districts. This past May, Rep. Rush Holt from New Jersey's 12th Congressional District introduced a bill targeting the military's failure to protect war-weary troops against this growing threat. Naming his bill after East Brunswick-native Sgt. Coleman Bean, an army veteran of two tours in Iraq who shot and killed himself at age 25 while suffering from post-traumatic stress disorder, Holt said, "Two federal agencies charged with helping prevent suicides among our returning troops utterly failed Sgt. Bean and his family."

Legislation to force a slow-to-react military establishment into taking preventive action is welcome, but are we treating symptoms of the problem rather than its cause? We need more men and women in the military, so overseas combat duty can be *part* of a soldier's or marine's service, not the multiple-deployment revolving door it is today. Unfortunately, as the two wars become more burdensome for the young people fighting them, recruiting new troops and retaining existing troops become more problematical.

An all-volunteer military is not going to cut it anymore, especially when one considers the potential need for military intervention in other hot spots—most notably, the Korean peninsula. Tensions are mounting there in the aftermath of a North Korean midget submarine torpedoing and sinking a South Korean ship, with the loss of all 46 men aboard. We are in the saber-rattling phase of that confrontation right now—an aircraft carrier has just been sent to the area—but President Obama's options may be limited. We just don't have the troops to fight on three fronts, and our enemies know that.

In 2006, a panel of prominent Americans, including former cabinet secretaries Madeline Albright (State) and William J. Perry (Defense), former Joint Chiefs Chairman John M. Shalikashvili, and former NATO Supreme Commander Wesley K. Clark, studied the whole question of a military stretched to the breaking point. While not calling for a draft as the final solution, the panel did come out forcefully for a new paradigm for national service. "We need to find ways," they said, "to bring Americans with critical skill sets . . . into national service of some kind."

FDU's Peter Woolley is also more optimistic about the viability of other national service alternatives, besides the military. "National service is different," he said. "It polls well, especially among older people. It polls well enough that national candidates have from time to time spoken of it aloud."

Nevertheless, Dr. Woolley sees problems in actually getting it done. "While many think it's a good idea," he said, "it hasn't advanced much. It's more attractive as an idea than as a piece of legislation. The details are hard work."

But since when has hard work deterred Americans? When have we buckled under the enormity of a task and decided *not* to pursue that task, one crucial to our national well being, because it was too tough? In his stirring inaugural speech, delivered fifty years ago at the height of the Cold War, President John F. Kennedy challenged our nation to throw off the bonds of self-interest and to "ask what *you* can do for your country." Americans, young and old, have always risen to meet such challenges. But they often have to be inspired and, more importantly, have to be *asked* to do the right thing.

President Obama and Congress: It is time to inspire us . . . and to ask us to make the sacrifices necessary to keep our country strong.

Chapter 3

One of my proudest duties as mayor of Ramsey was the privilege of speaking at our Memorial Day and Veterans' Day observances each year. When I left office at the end of 2006, that privilege transferred to the new mayor. But on Memorial Day 2012, the local VFW Post, which organizes these two gatherings, invited me to speak once again. I was tremendously honored and thought long and hard about what I wanted to say that day. I had in mind to speak frankly about the human cost of unnecessary wars and the failure of elected leaders from both parties to take that cost into consideration, but worried about departing from the usual content of Memorial Day speeches, the patriotic rhetoric associated with such occasions. I finally resolved to speak plainly and forcefully about what was in my heart.

My speech was well received by almost everyone. One resident would later complain to the local paper about my politicizing such a sacred day, but she was clearly in the minority.

The constituents I was most concerned about, though, were the members of the VFW Post, those combat veterans of World War II, Korea, Vietnam, and our more recent wars, seated before me as I spoke. I need not have worried. To a man, they congratulated me after my speech. They viewed it as I did—words that needed to be spoken, words that were as patriotic as any I could have chosen. I was so touched by their support that I crafted my speech into an Op-Ed piece for The Record, which published it on Sunday, July 1, 2012.

Putting Brakes on the Rush to War[6]

Most folks, if you give them time to think, would tell you that America's last *good war* was the Second World War. Coincidentally, it was also the last war we fought according to Hoyle, or to put it more precisely, according to James Madison . . . and the U. S. Constitution.

Article I, Section 8 of our nation's most sacred document—yes, more sacred and more fundamental to our freedoms than the Declaration of Independence we celebrate this week—gives Congress the sole power to declare war. Yet, the last time Congress voted a declaration of war was December 8, 1941, the day after the "date which will live in infamy." All

---

wars since then have been entered into by presidents of both political parties, according to their passing impulses. And not one of those *undeclared* wars has been worth the blood and treasure to wage it.

Someone in President Truman's administration invented the term *police action* to characterize the Korean War, without calling it a war. For 145,000 American casualties (33,500 killed, 103,500 wounded, 8,000 missing), it was every bit a war. But thus began the practice of *branding* America's participation in wars—softening them with noble-sounding names to claim a higher purpose than the facts would warrant, as though Madison Avenue focus groups had taken over the Pentagon. The examples abound.

President Ronald Reagan's 1983 incursion into Grenada, ostensibly to rescue American students, may have been necessary. Some saw it as an attempt to rescue American prestige, which had been battered in Lebanon just days before when a terrorist attack took the lives of 241 servicemen. Whatever the motivation, what was gained by calling that war "Operation Urgent Fury," as it was then dubbed?

President George H. W. Bush's 1989 invasion of Panama to oust Manuel Noriega became "Operation Just Cause." After the fall of the Berlin Wall and victory in the Cold War, the United States viewed Noriega, a CIA-paid operative who had helped us against Nicaraguan Sandinistas, as a pesky mosquito to be swatted. Who could object? We were removing a drug-trafficking dictator who was brutalizing his own people, a refrain that would become all too familiar.

Bush 41's "Operation Desert Storm"—the first Iraq war, to drive Saddam Hussein out of Kuwait—was the most cautious undeclared war in our history. General Colin Powell's strategy of overwhelming force, painstakingly assembled through a *real* international coalition, resembled a Category 5 storm as it swept over and through Hussein's troops. Bush, to his lasting credit, had the sense to declare "mission accomplished" short of reaching Baghdad, before we became stuck in a nation-building quagmire. If only that old adage about the apple not falling far from the tree were true.

Monica Lewinsky aside, we remember President Bill Clinton as the last president to balance the budget, but those of us with a military affiliation can't forget his initial blundering in foreign affairs. Ill-prepared to be Commander-in-Chief, Clinton launched "Operation Restore Hope" in 1993, a humanitarian effort in Somalia that turned into disaster. Forgoing the Powell doctrine, Clinton sent an undersized, ill-equipped force of 160 elite troops into the capital city of Mogadishu against an estimated 2000 to 4,000 Somalis. The mission was to capture a warlord who was frustrating the peace process, but the result was the tragic *Black Hawk-down* scenario, and maimed bodies of American dead being dragged through the streets. Our ignoble withdrawal from that country soon followed. Twenty years later, Somalia remains a land of competing warlords and a refuge for pirates.

The second Iraq war and the war in Afghanistan provide more topical evidence of misguided military forays without a formal declaration of war but with, once again, much consideration given to branding.

"Operation Iraqi Freedom"? Thirty-six thousand Americans killed and wounded, and for what? For Iraqi freedom? To create a theocracy masquerading as a democracy that sees Iran as its friend and a government and people that view America with hostility and suspicion? The initial justification for war was to destroy Saddam Hussein's WMDs, but, when no WMDs were found, that mission transmogrified into a war to remove a brutal dictator. With dozens of brutal dictators in the world, all abusing their own citizens, one must wonder how compelling the case is to remove one or two of them. Clearly, any such motivation for U.S. military action is self-delusional, at best, and utterly specious, at worst.

"Operation Enduring Freedom"? It is an insult to our intelligence when leaders glorify war by affixing a name with such transparent intention. Eighteen thousand Americans killed and wounded in Afghanistan, and for what? Certainly not to eliminate Al-Qaeda as a threat—that was done early enough to allow withdrawal with honor. Instead, we're engaged in a war to prop up a corrupt government, a war in which Afghans we trained and equipped turn on and murder Americans. Enduring freedom, indeed. In Afghanistan, a land that has swallowed armies of Alexander, Genghis Khan, Russian Tsars, the British Empire, and the Soviet Union. And, after remnants of each army leave, a land that reverts, unerringly, to its barbarous, tribal ways, its stoning of women, its repression of not only free speech, but freedom of thought, of ideas, of spirit. Just once, I'd like us to elect a president who has read a history book.

Combat forces will leave Afghanistan by the end of 2014, but recently President Obama committed non-combat support to the government of Hamid Karzai for ten additional years, until 2024. Does anyone doubt that, within a year or two of our departure, Afghanistan will once again be as it was before we got there, will be as it has been for millennia?

And what will have been the price we paid for these results in Iraq and Afghanistan? Yes, we got Saddam Hussein. Yes, we got bin Laden. But at a cost of 6,461 killed and climbing and of 48,253 wounded and climbing, not to mention the trillions we've expended, all borrowed against our children's and grandchildren's futures.

Stephen Decatur, a naval hero of the early 19th century, once toasted his beloved United States: "To our country," he said, "in her commerce with other nations may she always be in the right. But right or wrong, our country." That is surely the sentiment of all patriotic Americans, as we celebrate this Independence Day. We shall stick by our country, no matter what. But do we not give greater honor to our war dead and war wounded—those who gained our independence and freedom—by demanding that elected leaders think long and hard about the consequences before sending young people into battle? Wouldn't it be a Godsend if our leaders were wise enough to exhaust all alternatives to war *before* they embark on the horrors of war?

The Founding Fathers had it right: War is terrible, not to be entered into lightly. But if Congress allows presidents the unrestrained power to wage war, what happens to the checks and balances so basic to our system of government? One criticism of the Articles of Confederation, the predecessor document to our Constitution, was that it impeded the central government's ability to prosecute a war. Maybe that wasn't so bad, after all.

Chapter 4

As the father of two high-achieving daughters, I would be first in line to take a hammer to any glass ceiling that prevents women from reaching their full potential. The fact that women did not receive a constitutional right to vote until the19th Amendment was ratified in 1920 is a travesty, as is the failure of the Equal Rights Amendment to gain ratification, despite ten years allocated to the process. Yet, just as I am strong for women's rights, I am equally committed to holding women accountable using the same standards by which men are held accountable. This next piece, posted on my "In the Arena" blog on December 30, 2009, illustrates the point.

Combat Effectiveness, or Political Correctness?

Let's assume for a moment you are a military commander in a war zone and your ability to maintain sufficient troop strength is crucial to mission success. The strain on your soldiers from multiple deployments and too little time home with families is almost unbearable. Despite this serious set of circumstances, let's further assume a few soldiers are voluntarily and deliberately inflicting medical conditions on themselves that require them to be sent home, out of the war zone and out of your manpower planning. Some of these shirkers may now be filling critical billets and may be difficult to replace immediately, causing operational holes and putting other soldiers at risk.

As commander, would you be within your rights to hold accountable those soldiers who had used a medical condition, voluntarily incurred and avoidable, to take themselves out of the war zone?

Not too long ago, Maj. Gen. Anthony Cucolo, faced with this exact scenario, took action. He instituted a new policy for his troops. Henceforth, he said, any female soldier under his command who became pregnant while serving in the war zone would be court-martialed, *along with her male sexual partner and father of the unborn child.* Equal treatment, in other words, for both participants.

The general's order was not meant to apply to female soldiers who became pregnant while on leave at home with their husbands. It was not meant to interfere with their reproductive decisions made in that context. It was directed solely at those female soldiers on the firing line in Iraq and their male partners who participated in the irresponsible act of unprotected sex that led to a pregnancy.

The firestorm General Cucolo's edict ignited among women's rights groups was immediate and pervasive. I don't recall one media commentator standing up for the principle involved here, although I don't see how anyone other than closed-minded extremists could condone the conduct it was meant to deter. By the general's own assertion, the intended punishment was most likely a letter of reprimand and certainly not imprisonment. A court-martial has a wide range of punishments available.

Unfortunately, political correctness won out again. General Raymond Odierno, the top commander in Iraq, issued his own set of policies, overturning those of Maj. Gen. Cucolo, his subordinate, and taking away the right of unit commanders to make their own policy decisions—a right that had been in existence almost as long as the United States Army.

What happened to equal rights? What happened to the concept of women having all the privileges and all the responsibilities of their male counterparts in the military? I understand and support a woman's right to be in charge of her own body, but voluntarily becoming pregnant in order to get a ticket home from the war zone ahead of your male comrades in arms and before you are due to be rotated home? That is shirking, plain and simple. And, it deserves punishment for the woman and well as for the male who was complicit in the unprotected act.

I have a strong suspicion—no evidence, but an undeniable gut feeling—the White House was involved in this decision. I am not an Obama basher. I voted for him and still think he is doing a good job overall (but I'd give him a *B*, not a *B+*, on his first year's performance). The women's rights groups got to the president. I think he is normally someone who understands nuance and has the courage to do the right thing. Here, I think he succumbed to pressure from his political base, to the detriment of true equality for women and military effectiveness. I think the president failed us as Commander-in-Chief in this instance.

Chapter 5

My unwavering opposition to the Iraq and prolonged Afghan wars continues in this "In the Arena" blog post on October 1, 2010. What provoked the outburst was the on-going practice of news media to describe American casualties in a certain way.

Five "NATO" Service Members Killed

I don't know if you've noticed this subtle new way the Associated Press and other major news media have of reporting casualties in the Afghanistan and Iraq wars. I'm not sure how long it has been going on, but I am getting sick of it—the idea of calling dead and wounded American kids "NATO" forces or "coalition" forces. It's almost as though there's a conspiracy (I'm not a "conspiracy" nut, but the word seems to fit here) to somehow soften, if that is possible, the human costs of these two wars by *not* referring to the casualties as Americans.

What a mess those "nattering nabobs" of neo-conservatism got us into. Just picture where we were as a nation at the end of Clinton's second term. We had a balanced budget, no wars, and a bright financial future, with the potential payoff of our national debt within a relatively short time frame. I'm not a big Clinton fan—my kids got me his autobiography as a gift six or seven years ago, and I haven't even opened it. But you have to give the man his due.

Okay, then 9/11 happened on George Bush's watch. Forget the forewarnings he disregarded, the president was thrust into an unprecedented situation—one he actually handled well in the beginning. We had the support of the entire world, and Islamic extremists had the condemnation of the entire world. When we ventured into Afghanistan to clean out the Al-Qaeda training camps that spawned the 9/11 attack, countries we never numbered among our friends gave support. Iran, for God's sake, supported us in the beginning.

If we had stopped there—wiping out Al-Qaeda in Afghanistan and pulling out—can you imagine where we would be today in terms of American lives and wounded, or our status in the world, or our financial condition? I know—I am speaking from the benefit of hindsight, which is always 20-20; but our leaders should have considered the potential consequences. Didn't any of them ever read a history book?[7] Didn't any of them ever consider the old maxim—"the enemy of my enemy is my friend"?

There is never going to be a stable, Western-style democratic nation among the Arab countries of the Middle East. They are tribal cultures, with deep-seated religious and tribal animosities of more than a thousand years' duration. We are not going to change that, no matter how many lives and how much treasure we pour into the region. Afghanistan is a black hole, more primitive and more ferocious than we could ever understand. Didn't the 10-year experience of the Soviet Union in Afghanistan teach us anything?

Saddam Hussein was a bloody bastard, and we're often reminded that he killed thousands of his own people. Well, we relieved the Iraqi people of that scourge, but more than 100,000 Iraqi civilians are dead in the process. Are they better off as a result, or would they have been better left alone? Hussein was also a counterfoil to Iran. Yes, we took out his mythical nuclear capability, but we are now faced with a potentially real nuclear capability in Iran, unchecked by a hostile neighbor. The new Iraq we created is a friend to our Iranian enemy, which shares the Shiite version of Islam adhered to by the Iraqi majority.

Historians will sort this all out, I'm sure. I won't be here to read about it, when the time comes. I do hope, though, that when they tally up the cost of this mess, they talk about Americans bearing the overwhelming share of that cost. Yes, a few countries provided cover for Bush's "coalition" fantasy and, sadly, they lost some troops. But these two wars were America's wars, and Americans will be feeling the effects for decades to come.

---

[7] You'll see this reference a lot in my writings, based on my love of history but also respecting 18th century British statesman Edmund Burke's famous quote, "Those who don't know history are destined to repeat it."

Chapter 6

A previously unpublished essay, written on the one-year anniversary of 9-11. Unfortunately, the circumstances complained about are still true today.

A Time to Reflect

One year ago, Arab extremists murdered almost 3,000 innocent victims to show their hatred of the country they call "the Great Satan." The United States of America has not always pursued a perfect foreign policy, but we have usually acted with good intentions, as we demonstrated in World War I, World War II, Korea, and yes, Vietnam. Millions of American lives were sacrificed or tragically altered forever, not for territorial gain or economic advantage, but for democratic values and the principle of freedom.

And yet, one year later, Americans are still at risk when we travel by air, or when we simply try to live our lives in peace and economic security.

Airport workers were federalized to upgrade standards, but people still manage to board airliners with weapons. In a recent test of high-traffic airports, screeners failed to recognize simulated weapons 10 percent of the time—an unacceptable result, when just one-tenth of one percent failure could mean hundreds of lives. In what surely must be misguided adherence to political correctness, airport personnel employ a random search policy that results in gray-haired ladies from Sioux Falls, children and other questionable targets being singled out for close inspection of their persons and carry-on bags. At the same time, checked luggage goes into airplane baggage compartments without screening, a disaster waiting to happen.

The F.B.I. and C.I.A. seem preoccupied with protecting their own turf at the expense of protecting our homeland. Warning signals that individual agents in the field relayed to headquarters were ignored by superiors either too incompetent or too untrained to react. The imminent creation of a whole new cabinet level of bureaucracy, with its color-coded alert system and fuzzily drawn lines of authority, somehow doesn't reassure.

A different kind of terrorist—mostly white guys in $2,000 suits and $500 shoes, living in just slightly subdued versions of the *Taj Mahal*—threatens our economic health. Despite soothing words from the president and others in his administration, the stock market tanks one day and bounces the next, with no rhyme or reason to its gyrations. Evening news clips of a few corporate executives being led from boardrooms in handcuffs give small comfort to those who lost their savings. The errant businessmen soon make bail and, with their access to the very best hired guns of the legal profession, will likely spend no time in prison. Meanwhile, retirees and those nearing retirement have had to rethink plans they made for what were supposed to be their golden years.

Unbelievably, tax cuts for the wealthiest one percent of Americans, which may have made sense a year and a day ago, remain inviolate, even in the face of mounting budget deficits. When we as individuals suffer a crisis in our own lives—one with drastic financial implications—don't we readjust? Shouldn't the government be doing the same?

The promise by both parties to put the social security trust fund in a so-called "lock box" has been forgotten. New Jersey and other states struggle to cope with huge shortfalls, a struggle made immensely more difficult because of a discernable lack of courage among lawmakers to do the right thing. Elected officials from both sides of the aisle engage in partisan bickering and finger-pointing.

Caroline Kennedy recently published an update of her father's book, *Profiles in Courage*. If I were writing a book about today's politicians, I might entitle it "Searching for *Just One* Profile in Courage." It would be a book filled with mostly searching and little finding.

Chapter 7

Naval hero Stephen Decatur's famous loyalty toast is well known in the military, but not so familiar among civilians. I've used Decatur's sentiment over and over again in my writings—here to express my utter shock over a news report about the American government using Central American prison inmates in the late 1940s to conduct medical experiments. We need to "own up" to these rare but significant lapses in American judgment, and acknowledge such transgressions, if we are to retain our place in the world. This piece is from my "In the Arena: blog on October 2, 2010.

Our Country, Right or Wrong

If you are taking the time to read political blogs, Dear Reader, surely you know about the outrageous and inhumane actions of the United States government in Guatemala shortly after World War II. This disturbing news was just reported in the media yesterday and confirmed by officials in the administration.

In a government-sponsored, taxpayer-funded program, live syphilis and gonorrhea bacteria were transported in the late 1940s from a Staten Island, New York lab to Guatemala, where they were used to intentionally infect prisoners, prostitutes, and soldiers. The purpose? To see if penicillin would be an effective cure for those venereal diseases. In other words, the United States was using human subjects for medical experimentation without their consent or knowledge, and we were doing so at about the time we were prosecuting Nazis at Nuremberg for crimes against humanity.

Mercifully, the Guatemalan outrage lasted only a few years, but its discontinuance was not because of a sudden moral awakening. The Tuskegee medical experiments prove that. Black men in Alabama already infected with syphilis were told they were being treated for the disease, when, if fact, they were purposely not being treated so the progression of the disease could be studied. The studies went on for decades and only ended when the program was exposed to public view . . . in 1972, for God's sake. Within the lifetime of most of us, we were using black Americans for medical experimentation.

Was there a racial component to the selection of the subjects (victims would be a better word) for these experiments? Most certainly. Poor, probably illiterate Latin Americans, from the lower rungs of life? Poor, probably uneducated African-Americans, with a social status no one cared about at the time? Do you have any doubt?

Remember President Obama's speech in Cairo early in his presidency? The Limbaugh/Beck/Palin-wing of the Republican Party castigated him for having the temerity to admit to foreigners that America could have made mistakes in the past. How dare he? they said. America is never in the wrong, they said. America is Ronald Reagan's "shining city upon the hill," the world's moral compass, they said.

Well, that certainly is our self-image. Trouble is, the world no longer views us that way. And this latest disclosure of America's sordid medical experiments in Guatemala will likely perpetuate that negative view.

I am reminded of the toast Stephen Decatur once proposed to his shipmates. Decatur, an early naval hero most famously known for his actions against the Barbary pirates of North Africa, raised his glass and said, "Our country, in her intercourse with other nations may she always be in the right, but, right or wrong, our county."

I still feel the way Decatur did. But I wish the far-right fringes of our society would take a moment to reflect, now and then, on the notion that we are far from perfect. That we have made and still make mistakes—infrequently, I would hope, but mistakes nonetheless. It is not unpatriotic to acknowledge that fact. Not learning from our mistakes would be the greater tragedy.

Chapter 8

I've been an adjunct professor at Fairleigh Dickinson University for a dozen years, as well as an instructor at Rutgers and William Paterson Universities. Although I've taught a variety of subjects, including English, criminal justice, and history, my favorite and longest association has been with American government and politics. I've become a student, myself . . . of the U.S. Constitution, perhaps the most remarkable document in the history of organized human society.

The extreme right wing of the Republican Party is also a bastion of Constitution worshippers, but my beef with those tri-corner-hatted, flag-waving, scripture-quoting patriots is their selective embrace of our Constitution, their hypocritical, almost slavish, adherence to some of its principles while ignoring others. In this next, short piece, written for my "In the Arena" blog on January 4, 2011, a day before the 112th Congress of the United States was to be sworn in, I return to a familiar theme: Congress's continuing failure to assert, under the Constitution, its sole authority to declare war. It has left this terrible power to the president, alone. Together, the leaders of our country have consistently ignored the lessons of history to take us into one unnecessary war after another.

The U.S. Constitution—*All* of it Matters

When the new Congress convenes on Wednesday, January 5, 2011, the Republican majority in the House of Representatives will take up, as their first order of business, a reading of the U.S. Constitution. Rep. John Boehner of Ohio, who will be sworn in as the new Speaker of the House, has promised that exercise to remind elected leaders of the provisions of our great national document, the oldest written constitution in the world. I think that is a fine idea.

The purpose behind the Republicans reading the Constitution is clear. They want to emphasize the limited role of national government the Framers envisioned when they wrote the document in 1787, especially when it comes to controlling spending. They will probably have their first internal party squabble over who gets to read the Tenth Amendment, the so-called "Reserved Powers Clause" that was ratified in 1791 as part of the Bill of Rights. That brief provision reserves to the states and to the people all powers not specifically given to the national government.

It is a big deal for fiscal conservatives, as it should be.

But I just wish Republicans *and* Democrats paid more attention to the provision in Article I, Section 8 of the Constitution that gives to Congress the *exclusive* authority to declare war.

There hasn't been a congressional declaration of war since December 8, 1941; yet, from Korea to Afghanistan, this country has wasted tens of thousands of lives and hundreds of billions of dollars, not to mention the hundreds of thousands of seriously wounded U.S. troops and the millions of civilian casualties caught in the crossfire.

Korea looks the same as it did in May 1950, before the communists invaded the South, except it is worse now because of nuclear weapons at the disposal of the mad North Korean leader. If we had not intervened in that civil war, what would that peninsula be now? A united county with the industrious and democratic southern population in control?

Vietnam looks the same today as it would if we had not intervened in that civil war. True, a Communist country, but one that trades with us and that does not threaten our national interests. In fact, it is a buffer to China, its traditional enemy.

I could go on and on.

There is nothing wrong with attention being paid to our Constitution. I just wish it weren't so selective. And I wish that, once in a while, our national leaders would read a history book. They might learn that tribal cultures of a thousand years duration are likely to go on for another thousand years, despite our efforts at nation-building.

Chapter 9

I can't remember the last time I heard a political speech that didn't end in, "God bless you and God bless the United States of America." Frankly, I'm dismayed by the way religion now permeates our political discourse. If I could time-transport the 55 Framers from their Constitutional Convention in Philadelphia in 1787 to today's political arena, I think they'd share my consternation over what we've become, with regard not only to religious influence on politics and government but also to the complete disdain for the art of compromise. Here is my "In the Arena" blog post for August 31, 2010.

What Ever Happened to Article VI, Clause 3?

We are not supposed to care about the religious beliefs of our elected officials. That principle is embedded in the U.S. Constitution, Article VI, Clause 3, which reads, in part: ". . . no religious Test shall ever be required as a Qualification to any Office or public Trust under the United States." Yet, here we are debating whether President Barack Obama is a Muslim or a Christian.

A recent poll declared that 18% of all Americans were convinced the president is Muslim; 29% thought he was a Christian, and 43% didn't know what he was.

The president was forced to declare himself a Christian when this polling result displaced the dismal economy as the top story this week. When asked about this issue on a talk show, Sen. Mitch McConnell, the Republican minority leader of the Senate, said he took the president at his word. What I wish he had said, thereby turning this matter into a non-issue, is that it doesn't matter *what* religion the president practices or doesn't practice. What matter are the policies he is espousing and the effects those policies will have on our country.

Do you remember during the 2008 presidential campaign when Sen. John McCain was conducting a town hall meeting with an audience made up of mostly his supporters? A woman got up during the public comment portion of the meeting and referred to then candidate Obama as "an Arab." McCain quickly took the microphone from her and said, "No, that is not true. Not true."

I wish we had that Senator McCain back in the political arena. The "maverick" Senator McCain. The Senator McCain who wasn't afraid to be a leader on immigration, campaign finance reform, and a bunch of other issues worth talking about.

Instead, my former political hero has given us Sarah Palin, "build the *dang* wall," and an embarrassing display of far-right pandering. I guess he felt he was compelled to move rightward to overcome a primary challenge in his state. But he ended up winning handily, so maybe there was room for him to be the old McCain, if he'd wanted to.

This religion issue was a perfect time for Republicans and Democrats to point us in the right direction—the direction our Founding Fathers wanted us to take, embracing the freedoms in our Bill of Rights and avoiding "factions" and religious tests and all such hindrances to the rule of law.

There aren't many principled leaders in our country today in either party, it seems—the type willing to put country ahead of partisan politics. The type James Madison envisioned in Federalist #10.

It's discouraging.

Chapter 10

This piece appeared as the featured article in The Record's Opinion section on Sunday, April 14, 2002, and arose out of my experience in creating and teaching a death penalty course for Fairleigh Dickinson University at its Metropolitan Campus in Teaneck, New Jersey. That, along with my credentials as a prosecutor, got me this particular writing assignment, early in my association with The Record.

The article was so well received that I included it in my first book, Passion, Politics and Patriotism in Small-Town America. It has remained one of my most effective pieces of writing, and I now add it to this collection of essays, too, even though the death penalty was abolished in New Jersey on December 17, 2007.

Most readers assumed I was an opponent of capital punishment, but, in fact, my views on the subject are not that simple. I favor a limited-scope death penalty for the most heinous of crimes, like the rape and murder of children, with strict safeguards in its application and finality in the appeals process. But that's an essay for another day.

Rethinking Capital Punishment

On Monday Ray Krone stepped into the Arizona sunshine a free man, after twice being convicted of murder and spending the last 10 years in prison. Krone was sentenced to death in 1992 for murdering and sexually assaulting Kim Ancona, a Phoenix cocktail waitress. When that conviction was overturned on a technicality, Krone was retried before a second jury and again convicted, but this time his lawyers were successful in avoiding the death penalty for their client. Krone, who had spent three years on death row, was sentenced to life in prison.

The only significant evidence against Krone in both trials, according to defense attorney Christopher Plourd, was bite marks on the victim's left breast. Prosecutors at both trials presented the same forensic expert, who testified that the marks were consistent with Krone's crooked tooth structure. In other words, the expert said Krone made the bite marks.

"We presented three defense experts who testified that Ray's teeth didn't make those bite marks," Plourd said, "but the jury chose to believe the state's expert."

The jury was wrong both times. DNA evidence conclusively proved that another man, Kenneth Phillips, committed the crime. Phillips lived a short distance from the bar where Kim Ancona worked, but was not even considered a suspect at the time. He later was imprisoned for assaulting a minor and, under Arizona law, his DNA profile was added to a state data base. Krone's attorneys obtained a court order to search that data base using procedures not available in 1992, and Phillips' DNA proved to match the DNA left at the murder scene.

Prosecutors were so convinced of Phillips' guilt and Krone's innocence that they immediately went before a Maricopa County Superior Court judge to ask for Krone's release. A hearing is scheduled later this month to officially dismiss the charges, but it is a mere formality.

Ray Krone became the 100th former death row inmate to be released since 1973, according to the Death Penalty Information Center, a Washington, D.C., group that gets most of its funding from the J. Roderick MacArthur Foundation of Niles, Illinois. That same foundation also funds The MacArthur Justice Center, a non-profit public interest law firm affiliated with the University of Chicago Law School, and the American Civil Liberties Union—both fervent death penalty foes.

Richard C. Dieter, executive director of the Death Penalty Information Center, concedes that his group has been "mostly critical" of the death penalty as it is currently administered in the United States, but contends that DPIC's function is research, analysis and education. "We have not taken a position on the death penalty *per se*," he said in a recent interview. Yet, Dieter is quick to point out that problems with the death penalty over the last 25 years have not been fixed. "Arbitrariness and racial bias are difficult to root out," he said.

The 25- to 30-year time frame, roughly speaking, is generally accepted as the "modern era" in capital punishment jurisprudence. It stems from the U.S. Supreme Court's decision in *Furman v. Georgia*, a 1972 case that declared the Georgia and Texas death penalty statutes unconstitutional and, by extension, outlawed capital punishment throughout the United States. Georgia redrafted its death penalty law to address the Court's concerns, and that new statute, which passed Constitutional muster in 1976, became the model for 37 other states. But it could not be applied retroactively.

As a result of the *Furman* decision, 613 death row inmates in 30 states had their sentences commuted to life imprisonment by the stroke of a pen. Among them was Thomas Trantino, whose recent release on parole ended a decades-long fight by Bergen County law enforcement, politicians and residents to keep the convicted cop-killer behind bars.

Three of the *Furman* prisoners were later found to be not guilty of the crimes for which they were condemned to death. In other words, had the Supreme Court not acted, three innocent men would have been executed.

In New Jersey, news of the exoneration of the 100th wrongly convicted death-row inmate touched off a Trenton protest last week, with foes of capital punishment calling on state legislators to pass a bill that would stay executions until a study could be conducted on the death penalty's effectiveness. The bill is currently sitting in committee.

The prospect of a mistaken execution did not always alarm society's civil libertarians. John Stuart Mill, steadfast defender of 19th century British liberalism, argued in Parliament against a proposed measure abolishing the death penalty. Mill considered execution to be the more humane punishment, rather than a life sentence in prisons of the day. "[T]he short pang of a rapid death," he said, was less severe than confinement "in a living tomb." As for the occasional mistaken execution, Mill found the risk acceptable. "The man would have died at any rate," Mill said, "not so very much later on average . . . and with a considerably greater amount of bodily suffering."

Today, the execution of an innocent person is everyone's worst nightmare, pro-death penalty and anti-death penalty factions, alike. That may be the reason, perhaps, why Death Penalty Information Center's so-called "innocence list"—the running tally, now totaling 100, of inmates released from death row in the modern era—has attracted the attention of the media and public, not to mention the wrath of death penalty advocates.

"It's nothing more than a bogus public relations ploy," said Dudley Sharp, resource director of Justice For All, a staunch pro-death penalty group operating out of Houston, Texas. Harris County, Texas, and its political subdivision, Houston, are considered by many to be the death penalty capital of the United States. Its prosecutors have the distinction of consigning more convicted murderers to death row than any other county in the nation.

The Harris County D. A.'s office recently concluded one of the more notorious death penalty trials in recent years. It involved Andrea Pia

Yates, found guilty of murder in the drowning her five children. Mothers who kill their own children rarely face the death penalty. Susan Smith in South Carolina was another exception. Yates, with a documented history of mental illness, had pleaded insanity, but D.A. Chuck Rosenthal—elected, as all district attorneys in Texas are—said that "citizens of Harris County ought to be able to consider the full range of punishments in this case, including the death penalty." The jury that convicted Yates decided on a life sentence rather than the death penalty.

Some have speculated that D.A. Rosenthal's severe treatment of Andrea Yates, a middle class white, was designed to counterbalance the number of poor black defendants who are exposed to the death penalty in his county each year.

Justice For All's Dudley Sharp is the author of numerous pro-death penalty monographs, in which he attempts to debunk hot-button anti-death penalty issues like racial bias and mental retardation. One of Sharp's favorite targets is DPIC's innocence list. Sharp makes the point that most of the so-called "innocent" death row inmates on DPIC's list were released on a legal technicality, not because they were proven to be innocent. "This debate," Sharp says, referring to the dreaded prospect of a mistaken execution, "is not about legal innocence; it is and always has been about factual innocence, meaning, 'I didn't do it.'"

DPIC's list of 100 inmates released from death row is vastly inflated with "legally" innocent defendants, according to Sharp—defendants who may very well be guilty, but who got off because of a legal loophole. Nevertheless, Sharp allows that perhaps 30 factually innocent people may have been sentenced to death since 1973. If one considers that approximately 7,000 convicted murderers have received the death penalty in that time frame, 30 mistaken verdicts, or 0.4% of the total, is "an acceptable margin of error," Sharp said. Moreover, not one of these so-called innocents has been executed, a fact which Sharp offers as proof that the system works.

Richard Dieter concedes that "there hasn't yet been definitive proof of an innocent person being executed." But the DPIC executive director suggests that states have no incentive to open their evidence files regarding executed murderers. Many states, including New Jersey, require that evidence from homicide cases be retained indefinitely. It would be possible, theoretically, to gather DNA from a 30-year old murder case and prove conclusively whether an executed defendant actually committed the crime.

There's no percentage in states cooperating with an effort that may lead to their being publicly embarrassed, according to Dieter. Indeed, there is movement afoot in some states to outlaw inquiries into old murder cases with no living defendant.

Dieter downplays Sharp's distinction between factually innocent and legally innocent people on DPIC's list. "We don't just add a case because a defense attorney thinks his or her client didn't do the crime," Dieter said in a recent interview. He went on to describe the criteria his organization uses before a case is added to the innocence list.

A defendant whose conviction is overturned by a judge must be further exonerated in one of three ways: he must be acquitted at a new trial, or the prosecutor must drop the charges against him, or a governor must grant an absolute pardon. All 100 former death row inmates on the innocence list have been exonerated in one of those three ways, according to Dieter.

But Sharp doesn't buy it. "For death penalty opponents," he says, "the innocence issue has become but another distortion-based campaign."

Coincidentally, there is another list of 100 released defendants that has also received great public attention recently. Even Dudley Sharp seems to treat it with respect. The Innocence Project, a Cardozo Law School operation co-founded in 1992 by attorney and DNA expert Barry Scheck, has been instrumental in overturning convictions and setting free 100 wrongfully convicted men, accused primarily of sex crimes. This feat has been accomplished solely through the use of DNA evidence, which Scheck champions as highly reliable.

The relevance of Scheck's and co-founder Peter Neufeld's work to the death penalty issue is this. The 100 men freed by scientifically precise DNA evidence had been convicted by other evidence previously thought to be reliable. Evidence like eyewitness testimony, hair and fiber comparison tests, and even confessions by the exonerated defendants, themselves. In other words, 100 juries listened to victims identify their assailants, scientific experts render opinions, and police officers testify that defendants had confessed to them, then unanimously decided on the guilt of those 100 men beyond a reasonable doubt. And they were wrong 100 times.

Even fingerprint evidence, a previously sacrosanct law enforcement tool, has had its reliability questioned recently. U.S. District Court Judge Louis H. Pollak said prosecution experts could not testify that fingerprints found at a crime scene "matched" those of a defendant. In a ruling that could have had far reaching effects on the way criminal investigations and prosecutions are conducted, the judge ruled there was no scientific basis for experts to reach so definitive a conclusion as an exact "match." Asked by prosecutors to reconsider his decision, Judge Pollak reversed himself two months later. "I just changed my mind," he said.

DNA technology "points out flaws in the system," said Steven Hawkins, executive director of the National Coalition to Abolish the Death Penalty. Among the flaws Hawkins cites are "mistaken eyewitness identifications, unreliable jailhouse snitches, prosecutorial misconduct and exculpatory evidence that may come to light years after the crime."

Hawkins makes no claim of impartiality in the death penalty debate. His organization, founded with the support of the American Civil Liberties Union in 1976 when the Supreme Court reinstated the death penalty, has five thousand members and a thousand national, state and local affiliates. NCADP's one and only purpose, according to Hawkins, is abolishment of the death penalty.

Hawkins was asked whether the system was fixable. "That's the big question," he replied, pointing to no less an authority than former Supreme Court Justice Harry Blackmun, one of four justices in the minority when *Furman v. Georgia* was decided in 1972. That is, he voted to uphold the death penalty.

But in 1994, Justice Blackmun had a change of heart. In a capital case dissent, Blackmun wrote, "From this day forward, I shall no longer tinker with the machinery of death. Rather than continue to coddle the Court's delusion that the desired level of fairness has been achieved . . . , I feel morally and intellectually obligated simply to concede that the death penalty experiment has failed."

Justice Lewis Powell Jr., who voted with Blackmun to uphold the death penalty on numerous occasions, also expressed regret in 1994 over those votes. Powell told his biographer, "I would [now] vote the other way in any capital case."

Both Powell and Blackmun are long gone from the court, of course. But there may be further evidence of weakening support for capital punishment on the nation's highest court. In a July 2001 speech to an organization of women lawyers in Minnesota, Justice Sandra Day O'Connor, by her past decisions a firm supporter of the death penalty's constitutionality, said, "If statistics are any indication, the system may very well be allowing some innocent defendants to be executed."

Justice O'Connor was surely mindful of the situation in Illinois. In January 2000 Republican Governor George Ryan, a conservative death penalty supporter, declared a moratorium on executions in that state. Ryan's action came on the heels of hard-hitting investigative reporting by *Chicago Tribune* reporters Ken Armstrong and Steve Mills.

They examined all 285 death penalty cases in Illinois since capital punishment was restored in 1977. During that time period, Illinois had exonerated and released 13 men from death row, one more than it had executed. In a five-part series published in late 1999, Armstrong and Mills found "a system so plagued by unprofessionalism, imprecision and bias that they have rendered the state's ultimate form of punishment its least credible."

The reporters, who reviewed trial and appellate transcripts and interviewed witnesses, defendants and attorneys, learned that 33 defendants sentenced to die had been represented by lawyers subsequently disbarred or suspended from practice. In 46 cases, prosecutors had relied on evidence from jailhouse snitches, typically the most untrustworthy of witnesses. In 35 cases, a black defendant was sentenced to die by an all white jury, a result that could only have been achieved by prosecutors carefully skirting rules established by the Supreme Court to prevent such occurrences.

Indeed, 10 percent of all Illinois death penalty convictions had been overturned by appellate courts because of some form of prosecutorial overreaching—not the most ringing endorsement of a profession whose highest ethical obligation in every jurisdiction of this country is not just to convict, but to see justice done.

Yet, in spite of much recent coverage of death penalty errors, the public continues to support capital punishment by a significant margin. In response to a May 2001 Gallup poll question, "Do you favor the death penalty for those convicted of murder," 65% of respondents answered, "Yes." A post-September 11, 2001, poll saw that support rise to 68%, a relatively small increase considering the devastating loss of innocent life on that date.

Diann Rust-Tierney, director of ACLU's Capital Punishment Project, suggests that "the public supports the death penalty in theory, but the more the public understands how it operates in practice, the more that support erodes." Indeed, when life without parole is offered as an alternative to the death penalty, public support drops below 50%.

Ms. Rust-Tierney is right in one other regard. The death penalty is imposed in roughly 10% of cases in which the defendant has been declared eligible for capital punishment. In other words, when holding the life of a fellow human being in their hands—someone whom they have just convicted of a brutal, egregious murder—juries can agree unanimously to impose a death sentence in just one out of every ten cases.

Justice Thurgood Marshall put the matter more bluntly in his concurring opinion in the *Furman* case. The public supports the death penalty, he said, because it is ignorant of the facts. If the public only knew, he argued, that the death penalty does not deter better than long terms of imprisonment, that its implementation is inhumane and that it is administered unfairly, "the great mass of citizens . . . would conclude that the death penalty is immoral and therefore unconstitutional."

Justice Marshall's prediction has, so far, not been realized. Neither have Justice Blackmun's or Justice Powell's personal reversals on the death penalty turned the tide of public support. States continue to tinker with the death penalty in an honest effort to make it fairer.

Even Texas, the undisputed leader in executions since 1976, passed laws last spring, after former Governor George W. Bush's departure for Washington, to improve legal representation of indigent defendants and to mandate DNA testing in capital cases. The legislature passed another bill to block the execution of mentally retarded defendants, something 18 other death penalty states and the federal government now prohibit, but Governor Rick Perry vetoed that measure.

Recent efforts to improve death penalty laws, like those in Texas, are just "a drop in the bucket," says ACLU's Diann Rust-Tierney. "Why should we keep putting money into fixing the car when it's never going to run?" she asks.

Richard Dieter of the Death Penalty Information Center characterized this 100th exoneration involving Ray Krone as a "wake-up call," a warning that "states are taking unnecessary risks with innocent lives."

If recent statistics are any indication, the public appetite for the death penalty may, in fact, be subsiding. Justice Department statistics show a decline in executions two years running. After a modern era peak of 98 in 1999, executions dropped to 85 in 2000 and 66 in 2001. The number of death sentences being imposed by juries and judges, for that matter, is also declining significantly. Death sentences decreased for the third straight year in 2000, when just 214 death sentences were imposed, the fewest since 1982. The final tally for 2001 was not available as of this writing.

Eroding public trust in government and other once sacred institutions—like science, for example—may be spreading to the courtrooms of America.

The reality of junk science being used to convict innocent defendants came crashing down on even the most tough-on-crime advocates recently when the Federal Bureau of Investigation discredited the work of an Oklahoma City police scientist. Joyce Gilchrist had analyzed evidence in approximately 3,000 Oklahoma criminal cases from 1980 to 1993. In those cases, Ms. Gilchrist testified for the prosecution regarding blood, hair and fiber comparisons, matched results to defendants, and helped the state obtain countless convictions. Last spring, the F.B.I. said her work, either in the lab or courtroom, proved to be false in five of eight cases investigated.

Oklahoma Governor Frank Keating, himself a former prosecutor, ordered an immediate review of every felony conviction in which Ms. Gilchrist had any involvement. That process continues even now. Eventually, through new trials in some cases, outright dismissals in others, things will get sorted out, but the cost to Oklahoma taxpayers will be in the millions.

Another group will bear the greater cost, however. Scientist Joyce Gilchrist's testimony was instrumental in the conviction of 23 Oklahoma defendants sentenced to die by lethal injection. For 11 of those men, the inquiry into Ms. Gilchrist's credibility comes too late.

Chapter 11

Soon after the Republican National Convention in late summer 2008, when the world got its first look at Sarah Palin, I felt betrayed by a man who had been one of my heroes. How could Sen. McCain choose as his running mate a person so unqualified to succeed him? I thought. The move affected me so much that I wrote an essay and paid to have it published as a full-page ad in the Ramsey Suburban News, my hometown weekly newspaper, with the aim of letting my friends and supporters know where I stood. I could have submitted a letter to the editor for free, I guess, but I had much to say and didn't want to be constrained by the word limit for letters.

Like my father before me, I was active in Ramsey politics, having served as mayor from 2003 through 2006. I was elected as a Democrat, but during my term I threw off that party label and assumed the designation of Independent—much more suited to my own maverick-like, and McCain-like, brand of politics. The switch cost me re-election in November 2006, when the county Democratic boss put up a straw-man candidate to run on the Democratic line. I say "straw man" because the guy was practically invisible during the campaign—his only purpose was to siphon off enough votes to insure my defeat. It worked, and the Republican challenger eked out a win in the three-man race.

Sen. McCain would later recapture some of the esteem I'd felt for him. When a supporter during a town-hall style rally called Barack Obama "an Arab," McCain did not hesitate. He took the microphone from the woman's grasp, turned while shaking his head, and said: "No, Ma'am. No, Ma'am. No, Ma'am. He's a decent family man, citizen, that I just happen to have disagreements with on fundamental issues, and that's what this campaign is all about. He's not [an Arab]."

Here, then, is that essay from the Ramsey Suburban News, October 29, 2008, headlined with what I consider one of my best titles ever. Most of the headlines for my articles were chosen by my editors. This one was mine. The piece also has, in my opinion, some of the best lines I've written. See if you agree.

When Ambition Overtakes Honor

I was an early supporter of Sen. John McCain, not just this election cycle but in 2000. We are both Naval Academy graduates. Though we both wore gold wings on our uniforms as naval aviators, the similarity ended there. His exploits as a carrier pilot and his courage during more than five years as a POW are legendary. I had the much safer duty assignment as a patrol plane pilot in the Atlantic fleet, where no one was shooting at me.

My admiration for McCain grew during his losing campaign for the Republican nomination in 2000. Indeed, when I taught American government and politics at a New Jersey university in the early 2000s, Sen. McCain's "Straight-Talk Express" brand of politics was the role model I instilled in my students. Even when he strayed in South Carolina by condoning the Confederate flag flying over that state's capital, he redeemed himself later by admitting and apologizing for the outright pander.

McCain was a hero in the U.S. Senate, too, reaching across the aisle to propose bi-partisan campaign finance reform and a reasonable approach to illegal immigration. He opposed Bush's tax cuts for the rich as fiscally irresponsible. He was fearless in taking on "third-rail" issues that lesser politicians avoided, including religious leaders who sought to impose their own brand of morality on every American,

To win the 2008 Republican nomination, McCain veered to starboard. Perhaps he had no choice, if he wanted to win a nomination controlled by the ultra-conservative wing of his party, a reconstructed entity in which not only Rockefeller Republicans but also Eisenhower Republicans are as extinct as dinosaurs. Still, I stuck with him, generous with my contributions and loyal in my heart.

Even when he embraced those who had spread scurrilous lies about him in 2000 and, in fact, hired some of them to run his campaign, I accepted this as the "strange bedfellows" rule of politics. He was a pragmatist, I reasoned, and as soon as he was elected president, he would once again be his own man.

Now, sadly, I've come to the conclusion that I was wrong. His choice of Alaska governor Sarah Palin as his running mate tipped me over the edge. Palin may have mobilized his base, but it was the most dishonorable act of my former hero's distinguished career.

In many ways, Sarah Palin's career is an amazing political story. Her catapult to the governorship of Alaska, after brief stints as a PTA president, municipal council member and mayor of Wasilla (pop. 7,028) was Frank Capra-esque. But her placement on a national ticket as the Republican vice presidential nominee is Franz Kafka-esque.

Let anyone question Palin's qualifications—the complete absence of foreign policy experience, notwithstanding the proximity of Russia to Alaska, and her razor-thin resumé on just about every other difficult issue facing America today—and Limbaugh, O'Reilly, and Hannity, those nouveau champions of women's rights, bombard us with cries of sexism. If it weren't so frightening, it would be laughable.

The way McCain has conducted his campaign since he picked Palin is embarrassing. He is so heavily invested in attacking Obama's character that he fails to propose his own solutions for the real problems facing us. If ever there was a year for thoughtful, substantive political discourse, this is it. The Straight-Talk Express has four blown tires, and Sen. McCain has gone AWOL.

Once upon a time, John McCain was his own man, beholden to no one. Once upon a time, before the presidency became attainable and before that siren song reached his mariner's ears and lured him toward rocky shoals.

Barack Obama is a decent young man who has dedicated his adult life to public service. I don't agree with all his policies, but I like his earnestness and honesty. Although I am something of an *America-firster*, I recognize the need to be more diplomatic in our dealings with the rest of the world. Yes, we are the world's most powerful nation, but peace and prosperity will come through cooperation, I think, not confrontation. Obama shows a willingness to accept counsel and consider opposing views. He has the judgment and open-mindedness to be a successful president. Barack Obama will get my vote on November 4th.

Chapter 12

After the horrible tragedy at Newtown, Connecticut, on December 14, 2012, newspapers across the country devoted a lot of news-reporting and opinion space to the gun control debate. I weighed in with my take on the issue two days after President Obama announced a sweeping plan of action to deal with the crisis of gun violence in America. The following piece appeared in The Record on January 18, 2013.

Gun Control after Newtown[8]

In a news conference on Wednesday, President Barack Obama threw down the gauntlet on gun control. None of his initiatives was a surprise, but the scope was historic.

The measures—all require Congressional action, except 23 Executive Orders he signed—include reinstatement of the assault weapon ban that expired in 2004, banning high-capacity magazines and armor-piercing bullets, criminal record checks for gun purchasers, a new gun-trafficking law, and funding to hire more police. The government will address mental health by providing resources to identify and treat young people who pose a threat.

Nothing the president proposed will affect weapons, high capacity magazines, or ammunition now in the hands of gun owners. In other words, no confiscation.

Despite this safe haven for gun owners—the preservation of their personal status quo—the National Rifle Association and other pro-gun groups condemned the president's proposals. Not one measure the president put forth was to their liking. It was a continuation of the *slippery slope* mentality that has bedeviled gun advocates for years: Give an inch, they fear, and governments will take a mile.

NRA President Charlton Heston famously ended his speech at that organization's 2000 national convention with five words that have become a rallying cry. Holding a rifle aloft, Heston, in a voice Moses might have used with Pharaoh, proclaimed to the cheering crowd, "From my cold dead hands."

As a gun owner, NRA member, and Second Amendment supporter, I'd hoped for a less pedantic, more conciliatory tone from the NRA and other pro-gun groups. These massacres by mentally disturbed young men firing semi-automatic, military-style weapons with 30-round magazines have brought us to an emotional cliff, more perilous than any fiscal precipice. In what has become a national nightmare, we relive the horror with "Groundhog Day"-like repetitiveness.

Polls show that gun owners, if not their pro-gun organization leaders, may be ready to accept some restrictions. A poll of 45,000 gun owners taken in December 2011 by YouGov, a research group, found that 83 percent, and 77 percent of NRA members, favored keeping guns out of the hands of the mentally ill. These folks were less willing to accept a five-day waiting period to process background checks, but still, 60 percent of gun owners, generally, and half of NRA members were willing to go that far.

Sizeable minorities of non-NRA gun owners favored banning magazines with a greater than 10-round capacity (46 percent) and outlawing semi-automatic rifles and pistols (36 percent).

The NRA should be feeling more secure. The U.S. Supreme Court ended debate over the Second Amendment's ambiguous language tying "the right of the people to keep and bear arms" to a "well regulated militia" and came down on the side of individual rights. President Obama has stated his own belief in that interpretation.

Yet the Court left the door open for limiting gun rights. Even conservative Justice Anton Scalia agreed that the Second Amendment had a different meaning in 1791, when muskets capable of firing two rounds a minute were the weapons at hand.

NRA Executive Vice President Wayne LaPierre promised a "real solution" to the problem, but all we got was an untenable scheme to put armed guards in every school. Erich Pratt, spokesperson for Gun Owners of America, echoed LaPierre's solution. He called for "an armed teacher or principal" in every school.

Aside from the horrifying image of public schools becoming armed camps, the idea is simply not feasible. We must keep children safe, but will one person with a sidearm be effective against an intruder with a Bushmaster AR-15? Can you imagine a teacher or principal confronting that threat with a handgun?

So, where do we go from here? Will Newtown be just one more blip before we move on? Will the call for tougher gun laws run the usual post-massacre gamut of a month or so, then fade in the harsh political reality?

Perhaps the time is ripe to lay out a moderate program that is achievable politically but also workable. The old saying about *perfect* being the enemy of *good* applies. We must accept that America's gun culture is not going to change in the short term and may only be slightly alterable in the long term. But, to do nothing would be a travesty.

I don't think the president will succeed on the assault weapon ban, given the political reality of a House so gerrymandered that the only concern of Republican representatives is to avoid being "primaried" by a candidate to the right of them. But, even with that obstacle, there are things I think we can get done with the right approach.

First, let's end the name-calling. Epithets like "gun nut," which a New York paper used to describe Mr. LaPierre, do not advance the discussion.

Second, emphasize things most gun owners support, like eliminating the gun-show and private sale loopholes that allow gun purchases without background checks.

Third, update national and state records to provide searchable data bases, so those who should not be buying gun are readily identified, and vigorously enforce existing gun laws.

Fourth, let's wean kids off violent video games and do a better job of teaching them how to be more responsible citizens.

Fifth, we need to give greater attention to mental health, especially for returning war veterans, who are committing suicide in record numbers, and our youth. We're not doing enough to identify and treat those who are susceptible to this type of madness.

There are an estimated 300 million guns in this country, including two million Bushmasters. Congress will never enact a law to confiscate guns already in the hands of law-abiding citizens, notwithstanding the irrational fears of diehard survivalists. Criminals wouldn't comply, anyway. If such laws were attempted, we might just see Charlton Heston's admonition played out all across America, not in movie theaters but in the streets.

There has to be a better way, and I support the president's attempt to find that way.

Chapter 13

As this book goes to press, we are left wondering if Newtown will be just one more in a growing list of killings by deranged young men armed with military-style assault weapons. Or, will the specter of 20 dead 6- and 7-year-olds, each riddled with as many as 11 bullet holes, finally overcome the powerful gun lobby's opposition to even the mildest of reforms. In this featured Op-Ed piece, published in The Record on Sunday, March 24, 2013, you'll see why I'm pessimistic about anything substantive happening in this political environment.

Inside the N.R.A.[9]

So-called "common sense" measures, in the wake of the Newtown, Connecticut tragedy, came face-to-face with political reality this past week. Senate Majority Leader Harry Reid pulled a proposed assault weapons ban from the package of legislation he will submit to the full Senate next month, effectively killing the number one priority of gun-control advocates. As majority leader, Reid has that power and, clearly, he concluded that an assault weapons ban, the most aggressive measure under consideration, had no chance of gaining majority support, let alone the 60 votes needed to overcome a likely filibuster.

Sen. Diane Feinstein, principal sponsor of the assault weapons bill, could not hide her disappointment.

"I very much regret [Reid's decision]," Feinstein said. "I tried my best. But my best, I guess, wasn't good enough."

Frankly, it isn't certain that any gun-control legislation will make it through Congress.

After the horrible specter of 6- and 7-year-olds riddled by assault rifle bullets, one would think the prospects for enacting at least *some* gun-control measures were good. Even card-carrying members of the National Rifle Association support background checks to prevent people with criminal records or mental illness from buying guns.

Republican pollster Frank Luntz surveyed 945 gun owners in May 2012, seven months before Newtown, and reported that 74 percent of N.R.A. members favored criminal background checks for all gun buyers. Given Luntz's conservative bona fides, he surely did not rig poll questions to achieve a desired result.

In another poll, predating Newtown by a year, YouGov, a research group, found that 77 percent of N.R.A. members wanted to keep guns away from the mentally ill and that half of N.R.A. members would accept a five-day waiting period, presumably to complete background checks and close the gun-show loophole.

If a sizeable majority of N.R.A. members supports universal background checks, perhaps the least onerous of the current proposals, what's the problem?

Well, the problem is that the N.R.A. membership does not set policy for the N.R.A. That function is left to a 76-member board of directors—an inbred, closed society of believers in the slippery-slope philosophy: Let one gun control measure become law, no matter how benign or reasonable, and an avalanche of new restrictions will follow, up to and including confiscation.

No one gets a leadership position in the N.R.A. unless he or she adheres to the party line. Twenty-eight of the 29 board candidates this year were selected by the "nominating committee," which consists of nine individuals—six existing board members and three other N.R.A. "life" members—all selected by the board, itself. In other words, like-minded individuals perpetuating their power by replenishing themselves with like-minded individuals.

As a 12-year N.R.A. member, I'm eligible to participate—theoretically, at least—in the governance of this country's most powerful lobbying organization, but I had never paid much attention before. This year was different. Newtown, Connecticut, had made it different.

My ballot recently arrived in the mail, inviting me to vote for the N.R.A.'s board of directors. Each year, 25 directors are up for election to three-year terms, thereby staggering the turnover. But there really isn't much turnover, as most of those nominated are repeats—they've been serving and making policy for years. One additional board position, for a one-year term, is selected at the N.R.A.'s annual convention.

As I looked over the list of candidates in this year's balloting, a few names jumped out.

Ted Nugent, for one, a rock star and self-described "American icon." During a 2007 concert, Nugent likened President Obama to excrement, using the more offensive four-letter word, and invited the president to "suck on my machine gun." In that same diatribe, he called Hillary Clinton a "worthless bitch."

In April 2012, Nugent famously said at an N.R.A. convention, "If Barack Obama becomes president in November, again, I will either be dead or in jail by this time next year." While not a specific threat against the president, it was enough of a veiled threat to prompt the Secret Service to investigate Nugent. They declined to prosecute.

Nugent has been an N.R.A. board member since 1995. In his 2010 reelection bid, he was the second highest vote getter. Only fellow board member and war hero Oliver North, of Iran-Contra renown, polled more.

Larry Craig is on the ballot. Yes, the former U.S. Senator from Idaho, who was arrested in June 2007 in a men's room at the Minneapolis-St. Paul airport and charged with soliciting sex from an undercover officer. He eventually pleaded guilty to disorderly conduct. Craig used $217,000 in campaign funds to defend that charge, but the Federal Election Commission is now suing Craig over the use of those funds, claiming it was a personal expense.

Craig's lawyers, according to The Huffington Post, contend that it was a legally reimbursable expense because he was traveling from his home state to Washington, D.C., with a stopover in Minneapolis-St. Paul. "Not only was the trip itself constitutionally required," attorney Andrew Herman said, "but Senate rules sanction reimbursement for any cost relating to a senator's use of a bathroom while on official travel." You can't make this stuff up.

Pete Brownell is on the ballot. According to his official N.R.A. biography, Mr. Brownell is "CEO of Brownells, [the] world's largest supplier of gun parts, tools, shooting supplies, and ammunition." Is it any wonder that the N.R.A. vehemently opposes bans on armor-piercing bullets and high capacity magazines? Not when gun companies help direct N.R.A. policy and contribute millions to its "public information" campaigns.

Brownells, alone, gave more than $500,000 to the N.R.A. between 2005 and 2010. In his effort to become a board member, Pete Brownell made this statement: "Having directors who intimately understand and work in leadership positions within the firearms industry ensures the N.R.A.'s focus is honed on the overall mission of the organization."

George Kollitides, CEO of Remington Arms and Freedom Group, Inc., which made the AR-15 Bushmaster found at the scene of the Sandy Hook school massacre, is also on this year's ballot.

I don't doubt that there are honorable men and women serving on the N.R.A.'s board, including some of those cited here. But if anyone thinks the N.R.A. is going to be reasonable when it comes to even the most modest gun control proposal, he is sadly mistaken.

Republicans fear that a *yes* vote on any gun control measure, including universal background checks, will lead to them being "primaried" by an N.R.A.-backed challenger. Democratic senators up for reelection in 2014 in pro-gun states are not going to buck the N.R.A., either.

In the most stirring moment of his State of the Union address, President Obama called upon Congress to honor shooting victims in one particular way. Citing some victims by name and citing some by the growing list of geographic locales that have become our short-hand for this type of violence, the president said, *"They deserve a vote."* Over and over again, in the style and cadence of a preacher urging his flock toward the path of righteousness, the president said, *"They deserve a vote."*

The Congress of the United States, as we have so often seen, marches to the cadence of a different drummer. Meaningful gun control legislation making it through this 113th Congress is about as likely as N.R.A. Executive Vice President Wayne LaPierre becoming the next American Idol.

Chapter 14

Former Senator Rick Santorum (R., Pennsylvania) made a comment early in 2012, during the Republican presidential primary season, that astounded me. Referring to President Obama's stated wish that every child in American could go to college, Santorum said, "What a snob." Equating higher education with elitism, the far right has often been disdainful of learning. Santorum and his wife home-school their children, rather than subject them to the polluting influence of our public schools. One need not go beyond the religious right's view of creationism as science to understand this mentality.

This next essay, taken from my "In the Arena" blog post of October 27, 2010, illustrates the point.

The Importance of Being Ignorant

I teach American government and politics at a New Jersey university. Part-time. My students are mostly freshmen, with a few upper classmen. And they are mostly ignorant about their government and how it works—a condition I hope to remedy by the end of each semester. They are nice kids, and I forgive their ignorance, born of a texting, video game-playing, *never-read-a-book-if-my-life-depended-on-it* society. And high school curriculum choices that favor frills ("Today, class, we are going to make a *pesto* sauce to die for") and treat substantive content—reading, writing, math, and *civics*—like educational stepchildren.

What I can't forgive is the "Red Badge" of ignorance many of today's political candidates wear with pride. These candidates of whom I speak seem mostly on the *Tea-Bagger*-right, but if anyone can present an example from the left, I will be happy to modify my conclusion in that regard.

Christine O'Donnell, the Republican U.S. Senate candidate from Delaware, insisted in a televised debate with her opponent that "separation of church and state" was not in our Constitution. Regardless of her past dabbling in witchcraft, Ms. O'Donnell, like most Tea Party-endorsed candidates, strongly favors *more* religion in government and public life, especially religion of the Christian fundamentalist variety.

She wouldn't have had to look past the First Amendment, if she had the inclination and interest, to find one of the bedrock principles upon which the Framers built our system of government: "Congress shall make no law respecting an establishment of religion [or prohibiting the free exercise thereof]." Her campaign handlers later explained that Ms. O'Donnell did not misspeak. She was commenting on the exact words— "separation of church and state"—being absent from the Constitution and not on the principle embodied in those words.

In another recent debate, Jon Runyan, the Republican, Tea Party-endorsed candidate in the 3rd District of New Jersey, was asked to name a recent U.S. Supreme Court case with which he disagreed. After a considerable pause for the *endowed-everywhere-but-between-the-ears* former pro-football player to sort through his vast knowledge of liberal-leaning, activist-court cases the Tea Party abhors, he came up with his answer. *Dred Scott.* Yes, the pro-slavery decision handed down by the Roger B. Taney-led Court . . . in 1857.

Where is Nigel Bruce when we need him? You know—the wonderful actor who played Dr. Watson to Basil Rathbone's Sherlock Holmes. His favorite expression for any shocking occurrence was, "Great Scott!" I would love to have made that utterance immediately following Runyon's citing of *Dred Scott.*

In the latest poll, Jon Runyon leads his Democratic opponent.

I must admit that some Tea Party candidates, like Rand Paul in Kentucky and Joe Miller in Alaska, seem to be intelligent, principled, and knowledgeable, even if wrong-headed in some of their views. But the majority, I think, are the Sharron Angles and Christine O'Donnells of their House and Senate races.[10]

To what do we owe this state of affairs? To whom, I mean. Well, to Sarah Palin—that gun-tottin', master-of-the-Tweet, Mama Grizzly who will likely be the Republican nominee for president in 2012, with NJ Governor Chris Christie as her running mate.[11] Get ready for the solving of

---

[10] Today, I might have added the examples of Missouri Republican Senate candidate Todd Akin, who famously said that, in the case of a "legitimate" rape, a woman's body had a way of shutting down any resulting pregnancy and Indiana Republican Senate candidate Richard Murdouck, who said, in a debate, that if a pregnancy resulted from a rape, it was "something God intended." Mercifully, both Akin and Murdouck lost their races.

[11] A bad case of political prognostication. Palin seems to be fading in popularity, as evidenced by Fox News dropping her as a commentator. Christie, wisely, chose to wait until 2016.

all our problems in 140-character posts. Using my First Amendment right of "free exercise," I can only say, "God help us."

Palin's popularity rose, you'll remember, after left-wing media person Katie Couric asked her, in an interview during the 2008 campaign, such unfair questions as, "what newspapers do you read." After being blind-sided like that—you can't trust those media people—it became standard operating procedure for Palin, and the current crop of like-minded (I mean that in every sense of the phrase) political candidates, to shun media interviews, except with the friendly folks at Fox. Instead, Palin bombards us with Tweets, dutifully reported by even the left-wing media as though they were pearls of wisdom.

Maybe we need to blame another culprit for this fine mess we are in. The one my comic strip hero Pogo pointed out half a century ago: "We have met the enemy and he is us."

Chapter 15

NPR fails the political courage test. From my "In the Arena" blog post of October 22, 2010

National Public Radio—"Impotent, Limp and Gutless"

I never thought I'd be quoting Sarah Palin, but her 3-word characterization of the liberal media seems apropos in this case. National Public Radio (NPR) summarily fired its commentator, Juan Williams, for a remark he made in an interview with Bill O'Reilly, Fox Channel's resident "Bold, Fresh, Piece" of *something*.

Juan Williams, in addition to his former role with NPR, is also employed by Fox as a house-liberal in that bastion of conservative-speak, a foil to the likes of O'Reilly, Hannity, Krauthammer, Hume, Kristol, and Beck. He is Fox's tenuous claim to *"fair-and-balanced"*-ness. NPR had been getting complaints from its listeners about Williams going over to the enemy, so to speak. Williams was seen as aiding and abetting Fox in its journalistic posturing, and NPR was looking for an excuse to dump him. In his interview with O'Reilly, Williams gave it to them.

O'Reilly was trying to justify his recent anti-Muslim tirade while appearing as a guest on "The View," the daytime talk show that caters to smart women interested in current events. O'Reilly went overboard in his comments, even for him, and two of The View's panelists—Whoopi Goldberg and Joy Behar—got up and walked out in the middle of the show.

Anyway, in his interview of Juan Williams last Monday (I didn't see it, but have read about it), O'Reilly brought up the subject of Muslims, and Williams, according to The Associated Press, "talked about getting nervous on a plane when he sees people in Muslim dress."

Let me hazard a guess—I'll try to err on the conservative side in my estimate. Would you say that 99.99 percent of non-Muslim Americans "get nervous" when they see someone wearing the clothing of a Muslim fundamentalist on a plane? Okay, maybe I am being too expansive in my figuring. Let's tone that down to, let's say, 99.8 percent.

My point is that NPR canned an excellent reporter and commentator for the sin of being honest about the feelings that almost every post-9/11

American of non-Muslim heritage has. It doesn't mean we are bigots. It doesn't mean that our feelings are rational. It just means we are scared. Williams, in that same interview, went on to differentiate between Muslim extremists and Muslims who are as peace-loving and law-abiding as any ethnic or religious segment of America.

I am disgusted by the adherence to party-line talking points and ideology that both political parties usually exhibit. I hit the "mute" button during Sunday morning talk shows when the politician guests go into their lockstep routine. But NPR's firing of Williams goes beyond disgusting. It was a craven act by an organization that is supposed to stand for honest discussion and debate, an organization that is supposed to be the *real* "fair and balanced" forum in America.

Chapter 16

My on-going chronicle of the Sarah Palin phenomenon. "In the Arena," January 14, 2010.

A New Frankenstein Monster? You Betcha!

"It's aliiiiive," shrieks Dr. Frankenstein in the 1931 horror film classic, as he runs about his laboratory, driven insane by the sight of the come-to-life monster he created. I wonder if Sen. John McCain has similar feelings when he contemplates his own living creation—Sarah Palin, former mayor of Wasilla, half-term governor of Alaska (right next door to Russia), darling of the Tea-Baggers, book-touring non-author of the latest *New York Times* bestseller, and newly hired Fox News "analyst."

I was a supporter of and donor to John McCain's presidential campaigns in 2000 and 2008. He was a fellow alumnus of the U. S. Naval Academy, a war hero, and a damn good senator who wasn't afraid to reach across the aisle to get things done. We Navy types tend to stick together. I took a figurative front seat on his "Straight Talk Express" campaign bus and rooted for him from the moment he began his presidential bid in 2000.

George Bush's dirty-trick tactics in the South Carolina primary that year stopped McCain cold, but the feisty senator made a comeback eight years later and captured the Republican nomination. And then he committed what I consider the most dishonorable act of his long and distinguished service. An act that caused me to pull the emergency stop cord and get off the bus.

Just before the Republican convention was to open (and with his nomination assured), John McCain chose as his vice presidential running mate the most unqualified person ever to occupy a place on a national ticket. (Yes, I remember Dan Quayle, and I stick by my statement. Knowing how to spell "tomato" isn't everything.)

According to a newly published book about the 2008 campaign, 72-year-old McCain, on the basis of one meeting and a negligible vetting process, chose high-on-glitz, low-on-substance Sarah Palin to be a 72-year-old heartbeat away from the presidency of the United States of America. To be the potential commander-in-chief of our armed forces, in charge of two difficult and costly wars. To be the potential leader of the only remaining superpower in what has become a very dangerous world.

I haven't yet read *Game Change*, the provocative new book by John Heilemann and Mark Halperin that dishes on the 2008 presidential election campaign. According to published reports, the book overflows with juicy behind-the-scenes tidbits about the major players in that drama. Like the clumsy remark made by Senate President Harry Reid in support of candidate Barack Obama. Reid said Obama's chances were enhanced because he was a "light-skinned Negro" and could turn his "Negro dialect" on and off at will. Reid has apologized to the president, and the president has graciously accepted it and exonerated Reid of any implied racism.

To me, the most telling comments in the book, again as reported in the media, are about Sarah Palin's bursting upon the political stage. McCain had wanted Connecticut Senator Joe Lieberman as his running mate, but the Republican establishment balked at the idea of an independent Democrat on the ticket, especially a pro-choice one. Palin was put forth as an alternative by McCain's head political guy, Steve Schmidt. She was someone, he thought, who could ignite the base and give the campaign a needed lift. And, indeed, that is exactly what happened, at first. Palin did a good job delivering her prepared acceptance speech for the VP nomination, and the McCain-Palin ticket got a huge bump in the polls coming out of the convention.

But then, well, reality set in. You will remember that the McCain campaign went to great lengths to shield Palin from the media after the convention hullabaloo had died down. They had her under tight wraps and wouldn't let a reporter within 20 feet of her. She was not to open her mouth, except to say hello. Why was that, do you think?

Well, you saw what happened when she opened her mouth during the Katie Couric interview on CBS. Nothing of substance came out. Words came out, but their effect was like empty air, like the Cheshire Cat's smile transfixed in space as the cat disappears.

In preparing Palin for the debate against the Democratic vice presidential candidate, Senator Joe Biden, her handlers could not get her to stop referring to her opponent as "O'Biden." It was too demanding a task, apparently, to keep "O"-bama separate in her mind. Finally, they devised a strategy to avoid this embarrassment. They told her to ask Biden at the start if he would mind her calling him "Joe." We all heard her ask that on camera, and Biden graciously said it would be okay. So, Sarah Palin was saved from an embarrassing flub. Well, almost. She actually did refer to "O'Biden" once during the debate.

McCain's top campaign aides commented in *Game Change* about Palin's untruthfulness (a polite euphemism for "lying") in dealing with several issues that plagued her from the start, like her husband's proven membership in an extremist right-wing group that espoused secession from the United States and the governor's trooper-gate and expense-gate problems in Alaska.

Once he learned more about her, Steve Schmidt, her original champion in the McCain camp, couldn't believe her lack of knowledge about our government, American history, and the world in general. They had to conduct tutorials to teach her stuff most kids learn in elementary school—basic stuff like geography and civics. She didn't know, for example, that North Korea and South Korea are two different countries. South Korea is a democracy, of course, and our ally. Communist North Korea is one of the most dangerous places on earth, with its fruitcake leader, its nuclear weapons and its missile-testing frenzy.

We dodged a bullet with Sarah Palin. Sarah Palin is definitely "not smarter than a fifth-grader."

Chapter 17

This article was my first featured piece in The Record, appearing in the Sunday Opinion section on January 6, 2002. I'm proud of the way I was able to write about plagiarism, a serious problem in today's colleges and universities, while adding a touch of humor to keep the non-academic reader's interest. The piece remains one of my favorites.

I'd been teaching just two years, at three different schools, and was stunned by the prevalence of plagiarism. I treated every instance severely, either imposing a failing grade for the paper, if the offense was limited to a paragraph or two, or a failing grade for the entire course for more extensive violations. One student commented, in his end of semester evaluation of the instructor, that the thing he liked least about my course was "fear of being executed for plagiarism."

I included this essay in my first book and share it with you again, here in these pages.

Making the Grade

Students plagiarizing best term papers money can buy

I caught the first two culprits a year ago. I had been teaching only a short while, as an adjunct professor—a fancy name colleges give part-time teachers in lieu of decent pay and benefits. It was near the end of term, and students in my freshman writing class had been assigned a five-page essay. Two young ladies, both borderline C students, turned in A papers.

At first, I was delighted by what I read. Credit a master teacher at work, I thought. Then I read the papers a second time, focusing on a turn of phrase here, a clever word choice there, writing constructions students rarely use. Suspicious now, I spent the next few hours searching the Internet and, regrettably, found the true sources of both papers. One student had lifted her paper, verbatim, from an obscure article published years earlier. The other student, a bit more industrious, had patched together her paper from several sources. Both passed off another's work as their own. Both flunked the course.

I've read at least a thousand student papers and have acquired, I think, a feel for the way students write. For the most part, they stink. Not all of them. Only about 75%. The reason, of course, is that young people don't read anymore, and their attempts to write a sentence or paragraph show it. Half of them can't identify the subject or verb in a sentence. Try talking about agreement between pronouns and their antecedents, and eyes glaze over. They weren't taught these basic skills in elementary school, or in high school.

But they did learn the art of plagiarism. Why work hours on a paper when one can be generated effortlessly using the Internet? The potential rewards are substantial: better grades; higher class rank; acceptance into a more prestigious college; and, most important for some, parental approval. Chances of getting caught are slim to none. Nobody checks. If by some quirk a student is caught, punishment will be light. Our litigious society has turned school administrators into pusillanimous pushovers.

As a consequence, kids show up at college unprepared to compose a coherent paragraph, but armed with the certain knowledge they can get by their entire academic careers without the need to do so. Students need not rely on their own pilfering skills. There are dozens of dot.coms on the Web advertising research papers for sale. The going rate is about six bucks a page for a canned, pre-written paper, or 20 bucks a page for a custom job.

I typed key words TERM PAPER into my AOL search engine and turned up 32 Web sites of paper mill companies willing to sell me a paper on just about any subject. At Yahoo I found 50 more. Academic publications estimate there are at least 150 companies offering this service. With competition so fierce, companies use catchy names to target customers. For example, the fraternity brothers of "Animal House" fame would undoubtedly be attracted by the paper mill calling itself schoolsucks.com. Those seeking a more professional approach might click on termpapermasters.com or academicpros.com. A more secretive type might choose 007.com.

One company goes after students comfortable with their self-image: lazystudents.com. Need a technical whiz? Go to BigNerds.com. Or, papergeeks.com. "We have no social life," that company boasts. "Let's be frank! All we do is write research papers."

Students in a hurry because they forgot about an assignment due tomorrow can try duenow.com or fastpapers.com. Use a credit card, and a paper can be faxed or e-mailed within an hour. If graduate school admission is a concern and a student needs an A to help her GPA, genius.com is the choice. An A not good enough? Try a-plus-essays.com.

I clicked on speedyresearch.net, which advertised itself as "The Web's Best Source for Term Paper Assistance." I don't doubt the claim. The company provides a search function so students can browse through tens of thousands of term papers in its inventory to find just the right one.

You don't get to read a paper before buying. With clients predisposed to stealing other people's work, that would be economically unwise. But speedyresearch.net does give a brief description, including the number of footnotes, sources cited and pages. The company also rates the proficiency level of its papers, another shopping convenience.

I typed in key word LOVE, clicked the search button, and hit the jackpot—401 papers in inventory, all having something to do with "love." They ranged from a 66-page tome entitled "Analysis of Sex, Love and Death in the Fiction of D.H. Lawrence" to a more modest offering on "Love Canal," the New York hazardous waste site, I presume. The D.H. Lawrence paper was rated "AG", meaning it was "exceptional quality, graduate level." The price? A mere $396, not bad for what obviously would have been several months' work for a student. The Love Canal essay, nine pages and rated "A", the next lower level, was more affordable at $54.

I thought I'd try another topic and, with tongue planted firmly in cheek, typed in key words ACADEMIC HONESTY. It took just a moment for my electronic helper to report, "No products match your criteria."

Paper mill sites all have prominent disclaimers posted on their Web pages—the work, perhaps, of nervous lawyers. Speedyresearch.net's disclaimer said: "All our materials are sold for research assistance only, not as a finished product for academic credit." Sure. Wink, wink.

Understandably, administrators and professors have become almost fatalistic about plagiarism, but a few are fighting back. According to *The Chronicle of Education*, Georgetown, Tulane and the University of California are among schools that provide teachers with a service called Turnitin.com. A suspect paper can be scanned into the service, which then searches its own data base and the Internet for the source. Still, some educators feel we may have gone too far in efforts to catch plagiarizers.

In a November 2001 *Chronicle* article entitled "Forget about Plagiarism. Just Teach," Rebecca Moore Howard, director of the writing program at Syracuse University, warns that "we risk becoming the enemies rather than the mentors of our students; we are replacing the student-teacher relationship with the criminal-police relationship." We teachers need to examine our pedagogy, she suggests. "It is possible students are cheating because they don't value the opportunity of learning in our classes."

Ms. Howard also raises a mirror to a darker side of academia. Who among us, she asks, has not been guilty somewhere in our personal lives of omitting quotation marks, or borrowing a particular useful phrase without attribution?

Indeed, in March 2000 the president of Hastings College retired after being charged with plagiarism. In May 2000 a Duke University freshman researching an English paper caught the president of Wesley College in an act of plagiarism. The college president blamed the error on researchers working for him, but was forced to withdraw his academic paper. In July 2001 Texas A & M fired a professor for plagiarism. In August 2001 Trinity International University fired its law school dean for plagiarizing a law review article.

When our leaders—whether in academia, government, or society in general—engage in shameful conduct and then lie about it, it's not difficult to grasp why appeals to students based on honesty and integrity don't work. But students, adults after all, must themselves bear a measure of responsibility. In a March 1999 plagiarism lecture, Margaret Fain and Peggy Bates of Coastal Carolina University observed that "students have come to college to get a credential—a credential that will allow them to pursue a chosen career. How they get this credential might be less important [to them] than simply getting it."

I'm not one to give up easily, so when this fall semester began, I was determined things would be different, at least in my classes. Yes, I would strive to be the teacher and mentor my students deserved. But I would also insist on honesty in my classroom.

My syllabus for a government and politics class referred to the university handbook, which warns about plagiarism and describes in detail the dire consequences that could result. On the first day of class, I put my own spin on the subject. "Don't do it," I told my students. "If you do it, I'll catch you."

I didn't check their initial assignment closely. It was my first exposure to their writing, and I wanted to give everyone the benefit of the doubt. But while reading their second papers, at mid-term when I knew them better and had an idea what their individual capabilities were, I set aside a half dozen or so that looked suspiciously like plagiarized work. Twenty percent of my class!

I worked the Internet until 3:00 a.m. and tracked down four papers as outright plagiarism, lifted verbatim without attribution. I couldn't find the others, but suspect they were purchased from paper mills. My first inclination was to flunk the four students I had caught red-handed. I spoke to my department head and showed her my proofs. She was supportive, but told me she usually dealt with such matters less harshly, perhaps by failing students for the plagiarized paper, itself, or lowering their final grade in the course. Plagiarism was a reality of contemporary college life, she said. There were software programs designed to detect plagiarism, but no funds in the university budget to purchase them. She didn't elaborate, but I sensed that in the routine weighing of priorities, this university, like many others, had consigned the fight against plagiarism to its wish list. It's a shame, because a well publicized anti-plagiarism tool might have served as an effective deterrent. Speak softly, but carry a big stick.

I met individually with the four students, confronted them with my discovery of their dishonesty, and listened to their profuse apologies. They all came clean, so to speak. Faced with the prospect of suspension or failure for the term, all were close to tears. They begged for a chance to redeem themselves.

In the end, I relented and just failed them for the plagiarized papers, alone. It was, I realized, the practice among my colleagues to handle the problem in this fashion, and I didn't think it would be fair for my plagiarizers to suffer a harsher penalty than the plagiarizers in other classes. If a crackdown is in order, and I believe it is, the university must undertake an institution-wide program to educate faculty and students about plagiarism and, perhaps, to put uniform penalties in place.

Soon after the incident, I did conduct a teach-in with my own students. I wrote truth, honor and integrity on the blackboard and asked, "What do these words mean in today's society?" In the dead silence that followed, I'm sure they were wondering, has Professor Muti taken leave of his senses? What does this have to do with today's lesson? But then tentative hands went up here and there, and we began a period-long discussion of truth, honor and integrity. I eventually guided them to an exploration of their own ethical underpinnings, including the willingness among most students to plagiarize, apparently without the slightest hesitancy. Everyone does it, they said. No one seems to be checking, they said, except you.

I talked to them about personal honor, about the bond that should exist between teacher and student. I spoke about how they needed to be honest so their children would be honest. So our society would be honest.

I thought I reached a few of them and felt pretty good about the way I handled things. My ego did not remain inflated for long.

Later that week at another university, where I also teach and where my reputation as a hard-nose is equally well established, I noticed upon entering my classroom that one anonymous disciple of mine had taped a printed sign to the window. In a way, I admired its Hemingwayesque embrace of strong verbs, its eschewal of adjectival modifiers.

"Muty Sucks," it said.

They can't spell either.

Chapter 18

A bit of fun, from my "In the Arena" post on February 12, 2010.

Not That There Is Anything Wrong with Wiccans and Druids

> *News item, The New York Times, February 2, 2010: "The Air Force Academy has set up an outdoor worship area for followers of Wicca, Druidism and other Earth-centered religions. A double circle of stones atop a hill on the campus near Colorado Springs has been designated for cadets . . . to practice Earth-centered faiths."*

I am a Naval Academy alumnus. Perhaps you've heard of the Army-Navy game? And the rivalry between the United States Naval Academy at Annapolis and the United States Military Academy at West Point? Well, here's one thing most civilians don't know or understand. In every game in every sport, other than when we are playing each other, Army and Navy root for each other. We are brothers (and now, sometimes, sisters). We've been through the same grueling plebe year experience, enduring "shove-outs" and "come-arounds" and "uniform drills" and "greyhound races." (One day, I'll define those terms for you. For now, suffice it to say, they were unpleasant exercises conceived by upper classmen and designed to "build character" in plebes.)

We Annapolis- and West Point-types have always suspected the Johnny-come-lately Air Force Academy of being a bit weird. Their plebe year, if you can call it that, is a tea party, compared to what we went through at USNA and USMA. Both Army, the senior military academy, and Navy had been around more than a hundred years before Air Force arrived on the scene in the 1950's. The ivy-covered brick and stone edifices on our East Coast campuses were what a service academy was supposed to look like. Our uniforms of traditional Navy blue and Army gray were what uniforms were supposed to look like. And then, along come these fly-boys dressed in psychedelic blue uniforms with lightning bolt insignia and housed in their glass and steel buildings up in the mountains . . . well, you get the idea.

Now, it can be confirmed, thanks to a brief news item in *The New York Times*. Weird. What next? A shrine to Capt. James T. Kirk of the Starship Enterprise?

May they live long and prosper.

Chapter 19

A clever little piece, I thought, but it won't win me book sales down south. Here's my "In the Arena" blog post from January 29, 2010.

What Is It with Palmetto State Politicians?

Is there something in the air in South Carolina? Noxious fireworks fumes that accumulate in toxic quantities and waft their way to Columbia, the state capital? Has Pedro broken loose from "South of the Border" and become a political consultant?

First, we have the "family values" governor, Mark Sanford, disappear for several days, telling his staff he was going hiking along the Appalachian Trail. He went so far as to leave his SUV parked at a site used by hikers as a starting-off point. Later, we learn he was on a romantic tryst with his girlfriend in Argentina.

This guy was mentioned prominently as a future Republican presidential candidate. He was on John McCain's short list for the vice presidential nomination in 2008. Now, his political career is over, and all I can say is, "Thank God." We don't need someone with that kind of judgment making decisions regarding our national interests.[12] (Yes, I know. Thank God the lying Democratic jerk from *North* Carolina was found out, too. Some of those noxious fumes must have carried farther north.)

I often wondered why Sanford wasn't impeached. Not only was he absent from his post in a most irresponsible way, he also may have used government funds to carry on his two-continent love affair. But just this past week, I got my answer why the South Carolina legislature did not try to remove this man from office.

If they had, Lt. Governor Andre Bauer would have replaced him, and that would have been worse—far worse—than having Mark Sanford at the helm, with all his faults.

Here is the proof. Bauer is running for the Republican nomination for governor to succeed Mark Sanford. At a campaign stop last week, he was asked about the practice of providing free or subsidized school lunches for poor children. For many of these children, it is the only nutritious meal they get all day. Here is what Bauer said.

---

[12] As this book goes to press, Sanford has announced his candidacy for the House of Representatives in South Carolina's First Congressional District. He will face other Republican challengers for the party nomination.

"My Grandmother was not a highly educated woman, but she told me as a small child to quit feeding stray animals. You know why? Because they breed. You're facilitating the problem if you give an animal or a person ample food supply. They will reproduce, especially ones that don't think too much further than that."

Have you ever heard anything so mean-spirited, so utterly shameful? Dear friends and fellow citizens—I don't care what party you belong to or what your political beliefs are—you have to be outraged about a gubernatorial aspirant making a statement like that and being, in fact, the front runner in the race.

Since making the statement, which was condemned by far too few Republicans, Bauer has been all over the place. At first, he was defiant and refused to back off his words. Then, he said he was misunderstood—he didn't mean to compare poor people to animals. Finally he said he "should have used a different metaphor."

When I was living down south during my Navy days and going through flight training, we used a word to describe a breed of insect that seemed to infiltrate every nook and cranny, no matter how clean you kept things. I guess it was something in the air. We called the critters "Palmetto bugs." What were they? Cockroaches.

Chapter 20

This is not a book for Rush Limbaugh fans. Here's my rebuke of the conservative talk show host, from "In the Arena" on January 16, 2010.

Rush Limbaugh's "Heart of Darkness"

A few weeks ago, radio talk-show host Rush Limbaugh, while vacationing in Hawaii, was stricken with chest pains and admitted to a hospital. Fortunately for Mr. Limbaugh, there was nothing seriously wrong with him, physically. He emerged from the hospital in good spirits and held an impromptu press conference, declaring the American health care system to be the best in the world. The medical staff, he proclaimed, had found his heart to be in perfect condition.

Ironically, given Limbaugh's relentless attacks on "Obama-care" as socialized medicine and a government takeover, the State of Hawaii's laws regarding health insurance and delivery of health care services are probably the most "socialized" in the United States, and, as a result, more Hawaiians, proportionately, have access to health care than most other Americans.

In Limbaugh's case, though, doctors failed to detect what could cause grave concern about how the man's heart is, or is not, functioning. It is a condition know as *penuria de pectus*, a rare affliction most commonly found in the fair and balanced environs of Fox News and among cowboy-hatted, shotgun-toting older white men of mean spirit.

Penuria de pectus, or "lacking a heart" as it is known among lay persons, is characterized by a propensity to use natural disasters, devastating wars, terrorist attacks, and other calamities affecting the human condition to advance one's own agenda, political or spiritual. Two recent examples jump to mind.

The Reverend Pat Robertson, televangelist and former presidential candidate, disclosed in a television interview what he termed a "true story" and what he offered as explanation for the terrible earthquake that ravished Haiti four days ago. The Reverend said the earthquake was God's retribution for Haitian slaves entering into a "pact with the Devil" centuries ago to gain their freedom from France. Evidently, God saved up His wrath over that sacrilegious act and chose January 2010 to let loose His vengeance. Robertson offered no insight as to why this particular month was chosen.

The second example involves our friend, Rush Limbaugh. Acting with the comity and reserve he is known for, Rush did not go so far as to blame the earthquake on President Obama and his administration. That would have been quite a leap, even for him. But he did not disappoint his faithful listeners entirely. He did use the Haitian tragedy to accuse the president of using the Haitian tragedy.

"They'll use this [earthquake] to burnish their credibility in the black community, both light-skinned and dark-skinned blacks," Limbaugh said, the reference to skin shades an intended dig at Senator Harry Reid's off-handed remark during the 2008 election campaign. Limbaugh went on to warn his followers not to contribute to Haitian relief through the Red Cross link on the White House website, suggesting that the White House would use personal information gained (not explaining how the International Red Cross would be in collusion with Obama) for future political purposes.

President Obama's reaction to the Haitian emergency was swift, sure, and compassionate, in stark contrast to President Bush's dithering during the Hurricane Katrina emergency. ("You're doing a heck of a job, Brownie" may very well be the second most memorable quote of the Bush-43 years, right after "Mission Accomplished.") I think this leadership difference, apparent to the entire nation, drove Limbaugh to spew forth his latest diatribe against Obama. The only way, really, to attack a strong humanitarian gesture like Obama's is to attack the motive behind it, as Limbaugh did when he ascribed selfish political reasons to the president's actions.

I don't know if there is a Heaven, or a Hell, but if the latter does exist as a final destination for some of us, I do hope its depths go beyond Dante's Ninth Circle. The truly despicable, the irretrievably depraved—individuals like Robertson and Limbaugh, to name two—deserve a special place in Hell. The Twenty-fourth Circle, perhaps?

Part II

The *Real* Italian-American Story

Essays about a Proud Heritage

The *Real* Italian-American Story

The House on Carol Street

Mafalda Stella

Tribute to Hugo Milano

Tancredo's Credo

Sacked at Sixty

Chapter 21

The genesis of this essay is an obituary that caught my eye on Christmas morning, 2009. I couldn't wait to express the emotion and pride in heritage it aroused in me and sat down at my computer later that same day. Here's my "In the Arena" posting on December 26, 2009.

The *Real* Italian-American Story

This Christmas morning, I set about my usual routine of reading the papers—first, *The Record*, and then, *The New York Times*. It felt like a Sunday to me, sleeping late and having a big breakfast. But the papers were a lot thinner than Sunday papers and my favorite television news programs—*Sunday Morning*, *This Week*, and *Meet the Press*—were not on. So, I spent more time with the papers, including the obituaries.

Since crossing the age-60 threshold, reading the obits has become a habit. Before, I never bothered with them; now, I need to see if friends or acquaintances have died. As a history buff, I also read with sadness the growing number of entries that mark the passing of yet another World War II veteran. We're losing thousands each year.

As a boy in the 1940s, I remember reading an article in the *New York Daily News* about the last surviving Civil War veterans and lamenting the fact that Confederates outnumbered Union soldiers. There were five or six of the Rebels left and only one or two of the "good guys." Most had been 14- or 15-year old drummer boys. It's a wonder any drummers survived, marching as they did in the thick of every skirmish and beating a cadence to encourage their older comrades onward.

In 20 years, give or take, we'll be honoring the last of the World War II vets—all of them good guys.

I'm taking a long time to get to the point of telling you about one obituary I read this Christmas morning. It caught my eye because of its unusual length—two full columns in *The Record*. I don't recall ever seeing an obituary that long, especially since newspapers charge by the column inch to publish them.

Under a striking picture of an elderly gentleman who could have been the beloved father or grandfather of any of us, these words spurred me to read the entire obituary: "GIANNELLA, Silvio Vito – World War II Hero and Founder of the Giannella Baking Company in Paterson, NJ."

Silvio Vito was born in Italy in 1921, the youngest of nine children. His father Raffaelle, an Italian army veteran of the First World War (when Italy fought on the side of the Allies), had emigrated from their poor fishing village before Silvio's birth to seek a better life for his family in America. Italians who fought in WWI were granted visas to enter the US, but not their families. So, Raffaelle left his family behind, hoping to bring them over to the *new country* as soon as possible.

It would take 13 years. Raffaelle worked long, backbreaking hours in an Italian bakery in Paterson and later opened his own business, so that he could send money back to his family in Italy and still set a little aside each week—a fund that would eventually pay for their passage to America, wife Elizabeth and all nine children. Raffaelle also had to become a US citizen (which he accomplished in 1934) before authorities would allow his family to come over.

After the great influx of southern European immigrants during the late 1800s and early 1900s, mostly from Italy, United States immigration laws tightened, especially for the uneducated and unskilled. My own southern Italian grandparents, illiterate and dirt poor, came to this country in 1906 and 1907, before the exclusionary laws went into effect, thank God.

Once reunited, the Giannella family prospered. Their bakery business thrived and grew, with the children working after school and weekends alongside their father and mother. And, they became Americans. They certainly did not lose their love and appreciation for their Italian heritage, something I imagine they celebrated at every family gathering. But they became Americans, through and through. Let me tell you just how American they became.

On June 6, 1944, 22-year old Staff Sgt. Silvio Vito Giannella struggled through chest-high, blood-red water carrying 100 pounds of equipment and crawled up Omaha Beach in Normandy, just 20 minutes after the first D-Day assault wave had landed. Silvio was part of the Army's 6th Engineers, whose dangerous mission was to clear the beaches of mines and obstructions so that the tens of thousands of Allied soldiers could follow more safely.

In April 1945, half a world away, Silvio's brother, Fiore, stormed the beaches of Iwo Jima with the US Marines. It was the fiercest, most costly battle of the Pacific campaign. Fiore Giannella would die on those beaches, killed in action.

Silvio returned from the war and went back to the family bakery business. He would soon meet Sylvia Martelli, who became his wife and mother of his six children. Silvio and Sylvia, through their devotion to each other and their hard work, expanded the Giannella Baking Company, employing thousands of workers over the years. Silvio helped many of his employees start up their own businesses and sponsored dozens of immigrant families so they could obtain visas and experience the American dream, as he had.

Dear friends and fellow citizens of New Jersey, about 25 percent of us have Italian blood in our ancestry. We're the third largest ethnic group in this state. When you read headlines about mobsters whose names end in vowels and when you see movies and television stories about "Good Fellas" or "The Sopranos" or the "guidos" down by the "Jersey Shore," just remember one thing. Those stories are not your heritage.

The story of Silvio Vito Giannella, 1921 – 2009, a true American patriot and war hero—that is your heritage.

Chapter 22

A shorter version of this essay appeared in The New York Times on September 15, 2002, under the title, "The Un-Sopranos," a take-off on the hot HBO series at the time. Personally, I like my original title better and use it here, because of what the words mean to me. I often relate my writings to personal experience, especially my Italian heritage, and you'll see some of those same family references in this essay. It was my first published piece with this theme, and I remain sentimental about it, more than ten years later.

The House on Carol Street

The "fahgeddaboudits" and "howyadoons" spewed forth like staccato bursts from a tommy gun in HBO's mob hit, "The Sopranos." Tony Soprano and his crew put New Jersey on the map, but in a way that perpetuated an unfortunate stereotype. There is a different kind of Italian-American family saga that needs to be told, the one I experienced growing up in New Jersey in the 1940s and '50s. It was less exciting—everybody worked, nobody got *whacked*—but more representative of the 17 million Americans who proudly proclaim their Italian ancestry.

I live in Ramsey, New Jersey, a few blocks from the gray-stuccoed house on Carol Street where my father was raised. My grandparents had nine children. That number might have increased had my grandfather not died from a work injury in 1928.

My father Mauro Richard, the oldest son, became head of the family at fifteen. He was able to finish high school, but continued to work after school and weekends. All four boys in the family would eventually graduate from high school. Girls, in accordance with contemporary thinking, had no need for *higher* education. They went right to work after grammar school. Aunt Jean, the youngest, was the exception. She came of age when the family's fortunes were more secure and was allowed to attend Ramsey High School.

The family survived the 1930s, thanks to the indomitable spirit of my grandmother, an illiterate peasant girl from Calabria who stood barely five feet tall. I often wonder at her accomplishment. Left destitute with nine children and no husband at the beginning of the greatest economic upheaval this country has ever known, my giant of a grandmother kept her family together, reasonably well fed and clothed. Then, just as things began to look brighter, she sent three of her sons off to war.

Uncle Vince, seriously wounded by shrapnel while serving as a B-24 tail gunner, returned with the Purple Heart and multiple air medals to resume a career with the Ramsey Post Office. Uncle Tony, who fought with Patton's Third Army from Normandy to the Rhine, was highly decorated with medals himself, including the Bronze Star. He went to work for Curtiss-Wright building aircraft engines. Uncle Nick, a Navy man, became a bartender after his discharge.

My father spent the war years on the home front organizing relief efforts and keeping watch over his mother and family, as he had done his whole life.

My parents owned the Community Lunch, a fixture on Main Street for 16 years. In the Forties, they kept it open day and night to accommodate truckers and deliverymen. When both parents were working, I was dropped off at the house on Carol Street. I loved sleeping over in my father's old bedroom, barely large enough to accommodate its single bed.

I've never been able to fall asleep quickly, even as a child, and remember lying awake listening to crickets and frogs, unaware of the romantic purpose behind their nightly serenades. And, of course, the train whistles. I liked listening to the train whistles best of all.

Ramsey was a busy railroad town in those days. Hundred-car freights lumbered through regularly. During and just after the war, we'd see artillery guns and Jeeps strapped to flat cars. At times, stake-sided livestock cars were part of the mix, the protests of their hapless riders barely audible over the hypnotic clackety-clack of the rails. Freight cars fueled a boy's imagination with faraway names emblazoned on their sides—names like Norfolk and Western, Rock Island Line, Union Pacific, and, my favorite, The Route of the Phoebe Snow.

On winter mornings I could hear my grandmother in the cellar shoveling coal to stoke the furnace, whose fire she had banked the night before. The heat would make a racket as it rose in metal ducts, and I'd wait until I felt it escaping the floor vent before leaving the warmth of my bed. As I washed up, I could smell coffee brewing in the kitchen below.

I ate the same breakfast Grandma raised her brood on—toasted day-old Italian bread, buttered and dunked in a coffee and milk mixture that nowadays would be called *cafe latte*, but which we ignorantly called half and half. As a nutritional extra, my grandmother would crack a raw egg into a cup, spoon in sugar, add a few generous dashes of red wine, and beat the concoction vigorously with a fork. The result was an eggnog like no other. I don't know what its therapeutic properties were, but I've been healthy my entire life.

I remember vendors stopping by the house on Carol Street in rickety trucks or horse-drawn wagons. Some sold fresh fish packed in ice; others sold produce. One had a knife-sharpening rig, and Grandma would periodically take her cutlery outside to have edges honed. The iceman delivered once a week, carrying in a block on his shoulder after having chiseled it to fit the ice box compartment. On hot summer days, I always got a few mouth-sized chips to cool me off.

My grandmother's kitchen was large, rectangular and usually dark. I don't think the single electric light was ever turned on in daytime— a throwback to the time when a nickel saved here and there meant the difference between having enough food and going hungry. A white porcelain table was Grandma's workstation for weekly pasta-making and all other feats of culinary magic she performed in that primitive (by today's standards) kitchen. There was no cooking smell I liked better than my grandmother's meatballs frying in a large black pan on her old-fashioned stove. After the meatballs were drained, she gently dropped them into a simmering pot of tomato sauce, but not before setting aside three or four for me. She knew I liked them best in their crispy state, right out of the frying pan.

Inspired by Grandma's cooking, I once composed a 7th grade homework paper on her kitchen table using the family's upright Remington. Assigned to write an autobiography, I cockily titled my effort, "From Milk and Pabulum to Meatballs and Spaghetti, The Life Story of Richard Muti," foreshadowing my 60-year love affair with food.

My grandmother is gone now, as is my father, Aunt Minnie, Aunt Jean and Uncle Nick. Aunt Sallie, Aunt Rosie, and Uncle Tony passed just in the last twelve months. Only Uncle Vince and Aunt Josie are left. New owners have updated the family homestead, hiding its stodgy gray stucco behind vinyl siding. The two pear trees I used to climb have been cut down, and the grapevine-covered arbor my grandfather built is gone, too. A lawn covers ground where my grandmother's garden once flourished. In late summer, it was filled with tomato plants heavy with fruit, squash, Swiss chard and beets. It was also my favorite spot for digging fishing worms, the big night-crawler kind.

Now, as I lie awake at night a few blocks from the house on Carol Street, I no longer hear crickets or frogs outside. They seem to have disappeared, as these memories of my family will disappear when I, too, am gone. Trains, although fewer, still pass through town. When sleep is difficult, their whistles have the same lulling effect on me . . . and the power to transport an aging man, back along the route of the Phoebe Snow, to his childhood in Ramsey.

Chapter 23

Despite the fact that most of the essays in this book deal with public policy and national and state politics, I have also included pieces of a personal nature. This next essay is just that. One couldn't get more personal than the eulogy for one's mother. I managed to get through this when I delivered it at my mother's funeral mass, but just barely. I couldn't define my father, whom this book honors, without saying more about the woman he married. This is a short piece, and I beg your indulgence for including it.

Mafalda Stella

My mother was immensely proud of her unusual Italian first name. Her parents, Pia and Giuseppe Milano, named her after a then 17-year old princess, the daughter of King Victor Emmanuel III of Italy. Princess Mafalda of Savoy, although married to a German prince and Nazi Party member, opposed Hitler and the Nazis. She was arrested by the Gestapo in 1943 for her subversive activities and sent to Buchenwald. When the Allies bombed an ammunition factory near that concentration camp, Princess Mafalda sustained injuries that would cause her death.

Mafalda Stella Muti, of Waldwick and Ramsey, although not political and not of royal blood, was no less a heroine to the Milano and Muti families than her namesake was to the Italian nation. Her parents not only picked an appropriate first name for their third daughter, but they also chose a middle name that was propitious. "Stella"—the Italian word for *star*.

The Milano family was a matriarchal society, ruled by Pia Milano until her death in 1954. It wasn't that my grandfather Giuseppe was weak—far from it. He was a kind, gentle, hard-working man who was content to have his wife take charge of the household and their eight children. Soon after her mother's death and the death of her older sister Margaret two years later, my mother became the matriarchal head of the Milano family.

The Muti family had a similar disposition. My paternal grandfather, Sergio Muti, died from a work accident in 1928 just as the Great Depression was about to begin and left his wife Rosaria with no money and nine children. The Muti's, too, were used to deferring to a strong female. And so my father, who was a community leader in all respects, mostly deferred to my mother in domestic decisions. And those areas where he did not defer, my mother overcame by stealth and subterfuge, until her ultimate objective was attained.

My mother assumed her leadership role in her extended Milano-Muti families naturally, by dint of her strength of will, her work ethic, her unmatched energy, and her indomitable spirit that inspired awe and respect by all who came in contact with her. She had a forceful nature, which she often displayed with language, in both English and Italian, that would make some sailors I served with blush in embarrassment.

All six of the Milano sisters fancied themselves master chefs, having learned their craft at the side of their mother. And most of them were, indeed, excellent cooks. I say "most of them," because I once had a meatloaf dinner at Aunt Gen's house while I was home on leave that made me wish I were back in the mess hall at my Navy base. Aunt Margaret was in the restaurant business, like my mother, and could cook anything. Aunt Helen, who took loving care of her father, Giuseppe, until his death in his 90's, was also an all-around cook—top notch in everything, but especially baked goods. Aunt Corinne, or Aunt Tee, as we know her, is the gnocchi queen. Aunt Anita is also expert in everything, but I don't think anyone beats her ravioli.

While we were gathered around my mother's bedside, not long before she passed, Aunt Tee spoke words that were probably on everyone's mind. Turning toward my sister Rita, with sadness etched on her face, Aunt Tee said, in the most serious tone, "No more *pasta cheech*."

She was referring to my mother's pasta fagioli soup, which we called pasta cheech, for the chick peas my mother used in its recipe. My mother mostly stuck to three soups—pasta cheech, lentil, and minestrone—and they were my favorites of everything she made.

Speaking of recipes, none of the Milano girls, with the possible exception of Aunt Gen, wrote anything down on paper. The knowledge was all in their heads, learned as children from Pia, who also wrote nothing down.

My mother sensed she was dying soon after she came home from the hospital on New Year's Day. I never met anyone who fought a more valiant fight against cancer. With her strength nearly depleted and a physical therapist urging her on, she struggled mightily to stand and hold that position for a few seconds more, even as the therapist told her to sit back and rest. And she made attempt after attempt—"I want to walk," she said—even as the therapist told her to rest, that they would do more the next time.

A few days before she died, after she had become bedridden, I heard my mother say, "I want to see my mother."

"Who was your mother," I asked her, not sure if she was awake or just dreaming.

"Pia," she said.

In this beautiful church—the parish where my mother was baptized and married—perhaps we can hope, with God's grace, that Mafalda Stella Muti is now with Pia and Giuseppe Milano, her parents. And with her husband, Mauro Richard Muti and her daughter Rosemarie Creighton and her son John Anthony Muti.

As family members know, we are used to hearing at some point in the funeral mass, the voice of Hugo Milano singing the *Ave Maria.* Perhaps if we are silent for a moment, we can hear that beautiful voice still. And we can hope that Mafalda now sees again her brothers, Hugo and Queady, and her sisters who have gone ahead of her: Margaret, Helen, and Genevieve.

We are left a legacy of that Milano family in the form of Anita and Corinne, who mourn their sister's passing and who wonder how they will get along without her.

We all wonder that, but of course we shall all get along by the strength of our family ties—the glue that has kept the Milano and Muti legacies alive through poverty in the old country and through courageous uprooting by young Italian adventurers—Pia and Giuseppe and Sergio and Rosaria—to seek a new life in a strange land, whose language they barely understood and spoke but a few words.

I have copies of the ships' manifests for all four of my grandparents when they arrived at Ellis Island. Those documents give a tremendous amount of information, including how much money they had on them when they arrived. Giuseppe was the wealthiest of my four grandparents. He had $50 in his pocket.

Can you imagine the courage involved in such a move to a foreign land? That courage resides in most of you in this great church—it is in your blood. And it is up to you to summon it whenever it is required.

A few years ago, many of you attended the celebration of my mother's 90th birthday in the Adorno fathers' hall in Ramsey. At that party, my mother wanted me to invite all those in attendance that day to the celebration of her 100th birthday in June 2019. She had the spirit and the will to live that long, but the laws of nature will prevent her physical attendance at that party. Yes, there will be a party to celebrate the 100th anniversary of my mother's birth. My sister Rita and I will host that party, and, as my mother wished, you are all invited.

Mafalda Stella Muti
June 4, 1919 – January 24, 2012

La stella molto spectacola nel cielo.

Chapter 24

This is from a letter to the editor in the Ramsey Suburban News, shortly after the death of my uncle, Hugo Milano. He was my mother's younger brother and had married my father's youngest sister, and so, he was doubly related to me and doubly loved by me. He was the hardest worker in my extended family—a fact not disputed by anyone who knew him—and the hardest worker I ever knew. When I was a kid, I'd often see him come home late at night, bone-tired from the 12-14 hour day he'd just put in as a stone mason. I mean that literally—tired right down to his bones. Within an hour, he'd be so fast asleep on his couch that my Aunt Jean couldn't budge him to go to bed. This is a short piece, but when you read it, you'll understand why I could not exclude it.

Tribute to Hugo Milano

My uncle Hugo Milano died on June 13th, after a years-long battle with a virulent form of cancer that might have killed a lesser man in months. A week before he died, he was operating a backhoe, putting in trees at his daughter's new home in Mahwah. He was a devoutly religious man and sang in the choir at St. Paul R. C. Church in Ramsey. He was a member of the country club and, when he was well, loved to play golf. When the clubhouse burned down years ago, it was my uncle, a stone mason, who restored The Abbey, as it is known, to its original beauty, stone by stone. Hugo also loved surf fishing and would frequently pile children and grandchildren into his camper and head to the Jersey shore for that favored pastime.

But my uncle's passion was work. Although born in this country, he had an Old World work ethic inherited from his parents, both immigrants. He was taught his trade by an older brother and worked at it his whole life, well into his mid-seventies. It was back-breaking work, but I never heard him complain.

As mayor of Ramsey, I had the privilege to hear perhaps the greatest compliment paid to my uncle's craftsmanship. It came at a time when my uncle's last illness was becoming more incapacitating. I was sitting on the planning board, listening to a presentation by a prominent architect in town. The man was converting one of our town's old stone houses on Main Street to a commercial structure, including an addition. Someone on the board wanted to know if he would retain the stone facade and extend it to the newer sections of the building. The architect hesitated, and then said he probably couldn't guarantee that the stonework would be up to par on the addition.

"There is only one man I know of who could match the stonework on the house and make it look right," the architect said. "His name is Hugo Milano, but I think he's retired."

When I told my uncle about the architect's comments, he laughed and said, "You tell that guy to wait until I'm feeling a little better, and I'll do the job for him."

Chapter 25

Fortunately, Tom Tancredo no longer holds national office. This is from "In the Arena," February 15, 2010.

Tancredo's Credo

A Meanness of Spirit Walks the Land

Earlier this month, former Republican congressman Tom Tancredo thrilled the crowd at the "Tea Party" convention in Nashville by asserting, incorrectly, that Obama won the presidency because "we do not have a civics, literacy test before people can vote in this country." Mr. Tancredo, whose four grandparents were born in Italy, went on to add, "People who could not spell the word 'vote' or say it in English put a committed socialist ideologue in the White House—[his] name is Barack Hussein Obama." (When are these folks going to get over the man's middle name?) The gentleman from Colorado, who was the warm-up act for Sarah Palin's $100,000 speech to Tea-Baggers later in the convention, decried what he called "the cult of multiculturalism" in this country.

I am a product of American "multiculturalism," as is Mr. Tancredo. My four grandparents also emigrated from Italy. I've researched the Ellis Island records on line and have seen the ships' manifests when they arrived in New York harbor more than 100 years ago. The information awakened in me a new appreciation for what they encountered in this strange new land. And, a new pride in their courage and fortitude.

My maternal grandfather, Giuseppe Milano, was the wealthiest of the four—he had fifty bucks in his pocket when he arrived. My maternal grandmother, Pia Remia, came over as a teenager with her parents and sister. She had the most education and could read and write—Italian, not English. Giuseppe and Pia met here in the U.S., married, and had eight children—two sons and six daughters. Both sons served in the army during WWII.

My two paternal grandparents—Sergio Muti and Rosaria Potenza—were flat broke when they arrived, according to the manifests. Neither could read or write Italian, let alone English. My grandfather signed his name with an "X." They, too, met here in the U.S., married, and had nine children—four sons and five daughters. Three of the sons served during WWII—one fought with Patton's Third Army in Europe and another was a tail-gunner in a B-24. Uncle Vince was severely wounded on his 23rd bombing mission. He was awarded a Purple Heart and Air Medals with oak leaf clusters.

My family history isn't much different, I suspect, from that of millions of other immigrants, from dozens of countries. Almost all were assimilated into our culture, if not in the first generation, certainly by the second generation. Almost all became Americans as patriotic and hard-working as those with deeper roots in this society.

My four grandparents all entered this country legally, but that was a time when the United States still welcomed the world's "tired" and "poor" and "huddled masses yearning to breathe free." It was a time when this country needed unskilled laborers to perform the back-breaking work of building railroads and highways. Now, the only way poor people looking for a better life can get into the U.S. is to sneak across a border, or climb a wall, or brave shark-infested waters in leaky, overcrowded boats. I don't condone any violation of law, including immigration laws. But I also do not approve of withholding needed services from those who are here, or treating them like common criminals, like dirt. The type of xenophobic demagoguery uttered by Mr. Tancredo in Nashville gives me a sick feeling. I don't have a solution to this problem, but we need to find a solution. A humane solution.

Giuseppe and Pia and Sergio and Rosaria are gone now. They worked all their lives and were loving role models for their families. When they died, they still spoke broken English and, except for Pia, all were still illiterate and would have failed Mr. Tancredo's "civics, literary test." And America would have been the poorer for it.

Chapter 26

This article was published in The New York Times on Sunday, December 2, 2001, under the title, "Left High-Minded and Dry: Paying Dearly for Playing the Game of Life by the Rules." The piece relates to my experience of being fired in August 2000 as Deputy First Assistant Prosecutor in the Bergen County (New Jersey) Prosecutor's Office, a job and career I dearly loved, and to my attempt to regain my dignity and self-respect in the aftermath.

Writing this article and having it accepted for publication by a newspaper like the New York Times helped me cope with this painful time in my life. Because of its healing effect, the piece remains one of my favorites. I included in my first book and reprise it here. It closes out this part of the book dealing with my heritage—appropriately so, when one considers that it was my heritage that pulled me through.

Sacked at Sixty

I was fired from my job as chief administrator of a law enforcement agency two months after turning sixty—just 10 months shy of qualifying for health benefits during my retirement and two years shy of maximizing my pension.

My boss, a political appointee and head of the agency, wanted to spend $7 million of public funds to buy and renovate an office building. I had doubts about the need—we were having difficulty coming up with people and functions to fill the extra space. With the crime rate in a decade-long decline, we should have been finding ways to downsize, not expand. I tried to discuss these reservations, but my boss turned a deaf ear.

After a cursory review, the county governing body approved the project. I agonized, then was stricken with and succumbed to an attack of high-mindedness. I wrote county officials a letter explaining why the building wasn't justified and asking them to give it closer scrutiny. I got the ax that same day.

My wife took it hard. We'd just purchased another house, an old Victorian we fell in love with, and had not yet sold our existing home, so we were carrying two mortgages. "What are we going to do," she whispered, as I held her in my arms that first night. I told her not to worry, that I'd find a job quickly. But it was just whistling past the proverbial graveyard. The self-assurance I had always felt, the confidence that my abilities and work ethic would see me through, vanished that night.

I had always worked, ever since I was tall enough to operate the soda fountain in my father's small-town luncheonette. While in high school, I worked nights and weekends at the local Howard Johnson's. My dad's early training made me a star in that 28-flavor world. In college, I waited tables and ushered at movies and football games. While stationed ashore in the service, I sold encyclopedias door-to-door during off-duty hours, Navy pay being what it was in those days.

Putting together a resumé at the computer the next day, I felt my confidence return with each bold entry. Anybody would be nuts, I thought, not to want the guy I was describing on the screen.

- 1964 Annapolis graduate, B.S. degree
- 1964-69 Navy pilot
- 1971 Harvard Business School graduate, M.B.A. degree
- 1980 Rutgers Law School graduate, J.D. degree

I had 19 years as a lawyer, with over 500 trials and a win percentage in the high nineties, and fourteen years as a senior manager in business and government. I couldn't wait to get my resumes out. I'd need help, I thought, handling calls and sifting through job offers.

I was not disheartened by the lack of immediate response. But after enduring a silent phone for a few weeks, I decided to be sensible about applying for unemployment compensation. It wasn't something I wanted to do. I knew that it was an entitlement, that I had been paying into the fund all my life without drawing out a dime. Nevertheless, as a child of the Forties and Fifties, I couldn't help feeling a welfare-like stigma.

I pored over want ads. Tuesdays were best for *The Wall Street Journal*. Lots of executive positions suited to my education and experience. Sundays were best for *The New York Times, The Record and Star-Ledger*. At first, I sent out cover letters and resumés in those fancy Priority Mail envelopes at $3.20 each, hoping recipients would give special attention to my mailings. The phone remained silent, however, and I soon switched to the 34-cent method of communication.

Polite rejection letters began to arrive, with soothing words about someone fitting needs more closely and promises to keep my resumé "on file." Many didn't bother to respond. As more and more companies announced layoffs to cope with the worsening economy, I cringed at the new competition each cutback would represent. But I kept at it.

The Internet looked useful, so I registered at several Web sites. One, Monster.com, promised over 400,000 job openings. I put my resumé on line, headed with attention-grabbing words to lure employers who troll the data base. I used "Senior Administrator with Harvard MBA and law degree" as my hook. So far, 20 potential employers have looked at it. No phone calls, though. I may have to re-bait my hook. In a dark humor moment, I thought of using the ubiquitous Depression-era supplication, "Will Work for Food."

Recently, a friend, upset over my predicament, lashed out at me for what he perceived to be a self-inflicted wound. "What were you thinking?" he said. "Did you think anybody gives a damn about wasting the public's money? Why didn't you just keep your mouth shut, let them do what they want to do, and retire in two years with your pension and benefits intact?"

I often ask myself those same questions. When I recall the lessons my parents taught me and the values instilled in me at Annapolis and in the service, I feel proud about my actions, despite the personal cost. But late at night, when sleep is difficult and I find myself thinking about the sadness in my wife's eyes and her unspoken reproach for having thrown away our financial security over a selfish need "to do my duty," I am not so sure.

I've cleaned out the deferred compensation account I started years ago for our retirement. That old Victorian my wife and I bought turned out to have an unexpected feature. There is a bottomless pit in the rear yard, and every week or so, I have to go back there and throw money into it. While my fortunes may have taken a turn for the worse, I have been able to bring happiness to others. George, my electrician, and Tony, my plumber, and Rich, my carpenter, and Artie, my roofer, all had a very good year.

Part III

"Stop Me Before I Steal Again"

Essays about Public Policy

A Grass-Roots Victory

Should Towns Rein In Police Pay?

A Teachable Moment

Forsaking the Golden Rule

"Stop Me Before I Steal Again"

An Rx for Sick Pay

Losing a Say on School Budgets

The Death of 2+2 (and 1+3)

Public Employee Unions: Are They in the Public Interest?

Chapter 27

On November 7, 2006, I was defeated in my bid for a second term as mayor of Ramsey, New Jersey, my hometown.

In winning the office four years earlier, I had run as a Democrat in a heavily Republican town and had beaten a four-term incumbent by a landslide, carrying two council running mates, both political novices, into office on my coattails. But I would become disenchanted with the Democratic county political machine and its chairman.

On Sunday, April 11, 2004, The Record published my Op-Ed article titled "One Mayor's Declaration of Independence," in which I criticized the way the Democrats were governing at the county level and declared myself an Independent. And that's how I ran for re-election, as an Independent.[13]

I suffered an ego-crushing, though not entirely unexpected, defeat.

The Republicans ran a sitting councilman against me—a young, attractive, family man who actually supported most of the reform measures I'd initiated during my four years in office. The Democratic party boss put up a straw-man candidate, most assuredly to siphon votes from me, and the strategy worked. In the three-man race, I finished second, 189 votes behind the Republican challenger. The straw man, who hadn't bothered to campaign much and who was on the ballot simply to snare straight party-line voters, was a distant third. He had garnered about 800 votes out of 5,000 cast.

I left office on December 31, 2006, and accepted a full-time position as chief operating officer for a small company that sold diagnostic equipment to chiropractors. I also began putting together my first book, a compilation of essays and other materials I'd written, before and during my time as mayor. I made a point of staying out of local politics. The new mayor deserved an opportunity to lead the town without me looking over his shoulder.

But then I got drawn back into the arena by a series of events that are an instructive lesson and, perhaps, slightly tortuous guide on how local public policy can be changed for the better.

---

[13] The "Declaration" Op-Ed piece appears in my first book, *Passion, Politics and Patriotism in Small-Town America*, published through WingSpan Press in 2008 and still in print.

A Grass-Roots Victory

One of my major accomplishments as mayor was to curtail the rising cost of health insurance benefits for borough employees by limiting their choices to less expensive plans. When I entered office, the annual rate of increase for the town's insurance premiums was 23 percent; when I left office, it had dropped to five percent.

I was able to accomplish this because all five union contracts with borough employees expired on the day I took office, and I vowed not to sign any new contract that did not contain health insurance concessions. I also took personal charge of all negotiations, feeling qualified to do so by virtue of my prior service as chief administrator in the Bergen County Prosecutor's Office.

Early in the negotiations process, I issued a public statement that made my position clear.

> . . . we must take what will surely be an unpopular stand with our borough employees. We must learn how to say "No" to them, and it pains me greatly to have to do that. For the most part, they are wonderful, hardworking people, who have their own problems trying to raise families and make ends meet. But we can't keep agreeing to salary increases far in excess of annual cost of living adjustments, or to free medical insurance for the entire family.

The statement did not endear me to the borough's employees. In fact, it made many of them enemies and was a factor in my subsequent defeat at the polls. But I stuck to my guns and, by the time I left office, four unions had settled—all with health insurance concessions. The hold-outs settled soon after, with the new mayor being as firm as I had been on the need for concessions.

While mayor, I had followed closely the Ramsey Board of Education's struggles with its teachers' union, the Ramsey Teachers Association (RTA), even going so far as to attend BOE meetings and urging the trustees to take control of the burgeoning cost of health insurance benefits in the school district, over which they had governance, not I. (In New Jersey, school districts are separate governmental entities from the municipalities in which they are located.)

School taxes represented more than two-thirds of the property tax burden of our residents and, while, as mayor, I had no direct control in that regard, I was not shy about using the "bully pulpit" of my office to encourage the school board to act more responsibly in its labor settlements. Salaries and benefits for school employees constituted 70 percent of the district's $50 million budget at the time, and the only way my residents would begin to see property tax relief would be if the school board also learned to say, "No."

When the BOE began negotiations for a renewal contract with its teachers early in 2007, it began to show the backbone I had been looking for. Although the negotiations were secret at the time, I later learned that the BOE was insisting on health insurance concessions, but was willing to give good raises to achieve those concessions—something I was not opposed to in principle, so long as the long-term savings warranted it.

I watched in silence as the school negotiations played out over the ensuing year after I left office, but, when things turned nasty, I started attending BOE meetings to gauge for myself what was going on. And I didn't like what I saw. Finally, I could stay silent no longer. I wrote and published in the local newspaper, at my own considerable expense, a pages-long article that would, I hoped, rally the public behind the BOE's efforts to control costs. Here is that article, from the *Ramsey Suburban News*, June 11, 2008.

Taxpayer Alert!

A Call to Action from Private Citizen Richard Muti

Dear Friends and Fellow Citizens of Ramsey:

There is a struggle going on in our hometown right now, and I wonder how many of you are paying attention. I refer to the contract impasse between Ramsey teachers and the Board of Education. It may seem like a relatively minor affair, but I assure you it is not. The outcome will have long-lasting implications. I've not spoken publicly on local issues for 18 months, but this is so important to Ramsey's future that I couldn't stand silent. Please take the time to read on.

Before getting to the issue at hand, let's agree on this absolute certainty: Ramsey and other small towns in New Jersey face a bleak financial future. First, the State's finances have been mismanaged by elected officials of both political parties for many years. We have a mess on our hands, and things are likely to get worse. Second, politicians in Trenton lack the courage to deal with our problems. They propose measures that take a Band-Aid approach, while postponing the inevitable hard choices that must be made. They use gimmicks to balance annual budgets, like borrowing to meet operating expenses—a practice the NJ Supreme Court recently declared unconstitutional—or not making pension system payments for state employees. As a result, state debt and the pension deficit now exceed fifty *billion* dollars. Third, with New Jersey's finances on life support and with state "leaders" ineffectual, if not criminally derelict, in addressing problems, doesn't it follow that we must take steps at the local level to safeguard the future of our beloved town? Surely, everyone must see that.

State aid to municipalities and public education will shrink. It has been almost flat for the past six years, but you can expect sharp cuts ahead, especially for so-called "affluent" towns like Ramsey. It will start gradually: a five percent cut in 2009; then, 10 percent the next year; and so on. Five years from now, state aid to both the Borough and Ramsey school district will be 75 percent of what it is now, if we're lucky.[14] The burden to make up that revenue will fall on local property tax payers, of course. To survive, we must take control of our own destiny by reducing expenses wherever we can. Fellow citizens, if we are going to reduce expenses in our municipal and school budgets, we must look to where the money is. More than 60 percent of every property tax dollar goes to salaries and benefits of public employees.

Our school system and its teachers help make Ramsey a great place to live, but can we agree on a concept? I believe we can respect and honor our teachers, but still say this to them: "We will offer you good salaries and very good benefits, but you must accept the economic realities we face as a community. We'll do what we can to be fair, but please work with us. And please, do not use the children as pawns in these negotiations."

---

[14] We weren't lucky. In the spring of 2009, the state chopped one-quarter of its school funding for that school year. One year later, it cut 100 percent, and the school district was forced to cut 15 full-time positions. Half of Ramsey's school aid was later restored, but the future of state funding remains bleak.

There was a time when teachers were under-appreciated and grossly under-compensated. When I was a student at Ramsey High, I remember stopping at the Short Line bus terminal on Route 17 to catch a ride home after bowling at the Paramus lanes. Sitting behind the dispatcher's desk was my social studies teacher, working the night shift during school vacation to make ends meet for his family. I'm sure it was just one of several summer jobs he had to take. We should have taken better care of teachers back then, but I think we've gone a long way toward remedying previous neglect of one of society's most important professions.

Ramsey teachers now have decent but not great salaries for their 10-month work year. Actually, with school holidays, it is a 38-week work year (189 days). Each work day is limited to 5¼ hours of classroom time; but, to be fair, teachers also spend time preparing for class, counseling students, and grading papers, tests and other work. Salaries range from $43,000 for starting teachers with a B.A. degree to $95,000, but it takes 15 years and an M.A. degree plus 45 credits to reach that higher level. These are *not* unreasonably high salaries, especially when one considers the responsibilities inherent in the position—preparing children for *life*. I must also point out that under the current contract, a teacher with a B.A. degree and nine years experience earns under $50,000. Also, teachers, limited by tight school budgets, often spend their own money to enhance the learning experience for students. In good economic times, I might be an advocate to raise teachers' salaries significantly, but these are not good times. These are the worst of times.

Teachers' salaries may not be what we wish, but their benefits package is truly exceptional. They have outstanding health insurance, which provides coverage not just during working years, but in retirement, too. For the first three years, a Ramsey teacher gets just single coverage; after three years, we pay for the teacher's entire family. There's a $200 deductible per person and maximum $400 deductible per family. Coverage is for life, all at no cost to them. They also get dental insurance. Their pension plan far surpasses that of most private sector workers. Once tenured, teachers have almost iron-clad job security. And, there's a lot more.

Contract negotiations are confidential, so we don't know why the parties are at an impasse. I sense the main sticking point is health insurance benefits. I think the school board wants teachers to make a modest contribution toward health insurance (they pay nothing now), and teachers are adamantly opposed to doing so. Complicating the matter is the militancy of the New Jersey Educational Association (NJEA), the state teachers' union. NJEA has probably laid down the law to the Ramsey local: *Don't give an inch!* The reason? If the Ramsey union gives in and accepts even a slight reduction in health benefits, NJEA will view that as a "foot in the door" other school boards will try to emulate.

If Ramsey teachers were left to their own devices, without pressure from the state union, I think we'd have a contract. But that's not going to happen. In fact, Ramsey teachers have boarded the NJEA steamroller, much to my dismay. In March, I attended a school board meeting and was shocked at what I saw. More than 150 teachers and supporters, most carrying signs and chanting their "contract now" mantra, lined the high school corridors to the library, where the meeting was to take place. It was like running a gantlet, as this paper recently reported, and was clearly designed to intimidate and pressure school board members. There, in the halls of academia, where reason and civil discourse should prevail, I saw teachers resorting to bully-boy tactics. I applaud the school board for their courage in standing up to it. I felt intimidated as I walked to just that one meeting, but board members have been enduring it twice a month for quite a while.

What can we, the public, do to protect our interests? We can actively support the school board and encourage them to continue their reasonable approach to the health benefits issue, no matter what the pressure. We want them to deal fairly with teachers, but we want them to be firm. Costs must be brought under greater local control. Everyone—taxpayers and public employees, alike—must share the burden.

Let's make a public display of our support. Tell your friends about this article and then join me at the next school board meeting on June 24, 2008. Let's meet in the teachers' parking lot on the Main Street side of the high school at 7:15 p.m., and we'll walk the gantlet together. Let me know if you can make it. If you cannot join us on June 24th, write to the board beforehand or send an e-mail. Tell them how you feel about this issue. You can expect teachers and their supporters will respond most vociferously. Don't sit on the sidelines—let the people's voice be heard, too.

Thanks.

/signed/ Richard Muti

* * *

The article worked. Dozens of residents showed up in the parking lot the night of the meeting and joined with me in expressing to the school board our support for their firm stance. Many others wrote letters or emails. The recession had already begun, and folks in town were beginning to feel the pinch.

As it turned out, I was prophetic about the state cutting its aid to the Ramsey school district. Soon after he took office, Governor Chris Christie cut not five percent, not 10 percent, but 100 percent of the Ramsey school district's state aid, causing the district to lay off the equivalent of 15 full-time positions, mostly young, untenured teachers. The governor justified the drastic cut by saying that Ramsey and other towns like it could afford to absorb the cuts in aid, which the state could no longer afford to give.

Ramsey is a well-to-do town, but I would not put it in the affluent category that some of our neighboring towns enjoy. We have a lot of seniors living on fixed incomes and a lot of blue-collar folks just getting by, not to mention the white-collar workers who were, at the time, seeing their salaries frozen and their benefits—those that still had them, anyway— reduced.

Union leaders began ratcheting up the pressure on the school board. They continued their disruption of board meetings and, in an ill-advised move that would earn them the lasting enmity of many parents in the district, instructed their members to stop writing college recommendations letters for high school seniors. Still, the school board members appeared to be holding fast.

Encouraged, I spent hundreds more of my own money to publish another article in our local paper, this time to advise residents about the offer teachers were thumbing their noses at. It was a sweet deal that would, I knew, shock many in the private sector who were seeing further erosion of their own salaries and benefits. Here is that second article, which appeared in the Ramsey Suburban News on January 9, 2009, six months after the first article.

Here's the contract offer the Ramsey teachers' union is saying "NO" to.

A 4.5% raise each year, outstanding health insurance benefits for free, and $750 to $1,000 in annual dental coverage.

In addition, state law provides lifetime job tenure and an outstanding pension plan with free health benefits for life.

First, let me say that no one involved in the negotiations has violated confidentiality by talking to me. What I have, though, is information that is of public record and that shows conclusively, I believe, the substance of the offer the Board of Education has made to Ramsey teachers—an offer the union has rejected, causing prolonged unrest in our school system and detracting from the educational experience our students deserve.

When you see what the union considers inadequate, you will be outraged. This contract offer is such a sweet deal for the teachers, especially in this economic situation we find ourselves in, that one has to wonder whether the union is failing to disclose to its members what the school board has actually offered. Union leaders in the Ramsey Teachers Association and the NJEA have, I think, their own militant agenda, but, frankly, I just don't understand how the teachers, themselves, could put us through this turmoil if they knew what has been offered. About 80 percent of Ramsey teachers live elsewhere, but fair is fair. They should still care about our taxpayers and should still be reasonable.

Before I go any further, let me tell you how I can state with such certainty what the contract offer is. The teachers' union is not the only union in the district involved in contract negotiations. A separate union represents school administrators (the Ramsey Administrators Association) and still another represents teachers in supervisory positions (the Ramsey Supervisors Association). Both those unions have settled their contracts with the Ramsey Board of Education. In fact, I have at hand as I write this article the written Memorandum of Agreement for each. Those documents are public records and may be obtained by any citizen through the school board's office.

These two settlements are almost identical, and I would stake almost anything I own on the premise that the contract offer to the Ramsey Teachers Association follows the same methodology contained in the settlements reached with the Ramsey Administrators Association and the Ramsey Supervisors Association. The trustees serving on the school board are fair-minded men and women who love our school system and who would never, in my view, give one union a materially better deal than it offered to another union. As one who conducted public union negotiations from the management side for nine years, I know that just isn't done.

The Ramsey Administrators Association got a 4.54% raise in year one of their settlement, a 4.47% raise in year two, and a 4.43% raise in year three. Administrators gave up their right to choose what is called the "traditional" health insurance plan, to be replaced by a PPO health insurance plan guaranteed to be equal or better to the NJ State Employees Benefits Plan, with no additional contribution required. Administrators covered by other health insurance (through a spouse's employer, for example) can opt out of the Ramsey insurance plan and receive an extra payment of money equal to 30% of the cost of the Ramsey insurance plan. For example, if the Ramsey PPO insurance costs the school board $10,000 per employee, the employee has the option to choose *not* to be covered in Ramsey. If that option is selected by the employee, he or she gets $3,000 cash for making that choice. (If the spouse loses coverage, the Ramsey employee can get back into the Ramsey plan.) In addition, the school board will contribute toward the cost of dental insurance up to $750 in year one, up to $900 in year two, and up to $1,000 in year three. All other terms of the prior contract remain in effect.

The Ramsey Supervisors Association's settlement is almost exactly the same as the Administrators. They got a 4.52% raise in year one, instead of 4.54%. That is the only difference, as far as I can tell from reading both documents.

Well, there you have it. The Ramsey Teachers Association is rejecting annual raises in the range of 4.5% for their life-tenured members, at a time when hundreds of thousands of New Jersey residents have lost their jobs and when Ramsey taxpayers are struggling to cope with rising costs. Teachers are being asked to give up their free 24-karat gold "traditional" health insurance plan to accept, instead, a free 18-karat gold PPO health insurance plan—at a time when hundreds of thousands of New Jersey residents and many Ramsey residents have absolutely no health insurance coverage at all.

By the way, every Borough employee has the PPO plan, which is a wonderful benefit superior to what 95 percent of us in the private sector have. The last traditional plan hold-out in the Borough was the Ramsey police union. I ended that disparity during my first year as mayor, with support of the council. The PPO plan for teachers will save Ramsey taxpayers at least $500,000 a year.[15] I know that for certain, because

---

[15] I was mistaken in this estimate. The potential savings were much less.

when we moved Borough police away from the traditional plan, we saved $100,000 a year, and that was with only 32 police officers.

Fellow citizens, you know I have not always agreed with the school trustees. I never questioned their honesty and dedication, but there were times in the past when I didn't agree with their decisions. In these contract negotiations, they are, in my opinion, entirely in the right. I am not anti-teacher. I am a product of the Ramsey school system, K-12, and I still remember and revere my teachers, to whom I owe much. But in this matter, Ramsey teachers are in the wrong.

I urge you to support the school board, and to please let them know of your support. It isn't easy standing up to public employee unions. I know that from experience, too.

* * *

New Jersey is a pro-union state, especially so when it comes to public employee unions and most especially so when it comes to the New Jersey Education Association (NJEA), the statewide teachers' union. Over the years, NJEA has succeeded in getting laws and regulations enacted that give its local members a hammerlock over the school boards they negotiate with. A teachers' union can hold out for years and not accept any changes to its benefits, and the school board is powerless to do anything about it because, under the law, teachers will continue to get indefinitely the same benefits that were in place under their expired contract. And they continue to draw their salaries, which state law does not allow to be reduced.

If a contract impasse is declared, a state mediator is brought in to try to broker a deal. If that fails, a state fact-finder is brought in to take testimony from both sides and to issue a non-binding report as to his or her findings. If the fact-finder's report doesn't bring a resolution, then "super mediation" is the next step. If that, too, fails, the process just goes on and on, repeating itself until one side gives in.

The side that gives in is almost never the public union side. And, indeed, that is what happened in Ramsey. In late January 2009, the state fact-finder's report was made public, 10 days after BOE members had reviewed it. The fact-finder had recommended a four-year settlement, with annual raises of 4.2%, 4.2%, 4.2%, and 4.35%—16.95% in total—and no health insurance concessions on the part of the union.

Weary of the two-year-long fight, the Ramsey Board of Education caved to the pressure (I'm sorry—there is no other way I can describe it) and embraced the fact-finder's report. The RTA—which hadn't given

104

an insurance concession in 12 years, while the cost to taxpayers for those benefits had probably tripled—readily accepted the fact-finder's recommendations, too, and a deal was struck.

I was outraged by the school board's short-sightedness. I understood its desire to end a bitter labor dispute, but saw the settlement as not only the board's proverbial kicking of the can down the road, but also a grave threat to the future financial health of the district. I wrote still another article for publication in the local paper at my own expense.

The article was an indictment of the cozy relationship between the NJEA and New Jersey lawmakers and the havoc that relationship wreaked on municipalities and school districts and taxpayers throughout the state. It was also sharply critical of the Ramsey school board. In a sidebar at the end of the article, headlined "Attention Ramsey Property Tax Payers," I called for wholesale changes on the Ramsey Board of Education, but disclaimed, sincerely, any personal interest in running for a seat on the board. Here is that third article in this series, from the Ramsey Suburban News, February 18, 2009. Its headline is a play on a New Jersey tourism slogan of the time: "New Jersey and You – Perfect Together."

NJEA and the N. J. State Legislature – Perfect Together

Why have state legislators allowed public employee unions to get so powerful?
To borrow a line from *All the President's Men*, "follow the money."

The New Jersey Education Association (NJEA) is the most dominant force in the dirty arena of New Jersey politics, yet its public face is benevolent. For one thing, it represents employees we revere for their dedication to children. You've seen NJEA's television commercials—they portray everyone's ideal teacher. How can you not like these folks?

But take a look behind the scene.

There are 40 legislative districts in New Jersey, each represented by one senator and two assembly members—120 state legislators who are supposed to be looking out for *our* interests. Instead, they are in the pocket of the NJEA, bought and paid for. The proof is readily available through public records, accessible online at www.elec.state.nj.us.

I reviewed political contributions for 2003–2007, compiled from campaign reports filed with the NJ Election Law Enforcement Commission. Over that five-year period, NJEA and NJEA PAC, its political action committee, doled out $1,437,500 to state senate and assembly candidates, or $11,979 for every legislative seat. No other organization contributed as much.

NJEA gave to Democratic candidates in 26 legislative districts and to Republican candidates in 21 legislative districts. Yes, in seven districts they shrewdly gave to both sides. Money went to at least one candidate in every district.

You have to keep in mind that legislative districts in New Jersey have been so gerrymandered over the years that almost all are election *locks* for one party or the other. The Pillsbury Doughboy could run in most districts with the correct party label and get elected. Only a handful of districts have legitimate contests each election cycle.

Still, NJEA poured tens of thousands into safe districts held by committee chairs and other movers and shakers in Trenton, just to curry favor with people who control what legislation will reach the floor for a vote and how those votes will be cast.

This open-spigot political strategy of NJEA has paid off handsomely for New Jersey teachers, to the great detriment of the public. It is a pay-to-play scheme more costly to local property tax payers than anything party bosses in their Hugo Bosses ever dreamed of. Personnel costs make up 60-70% of school budgets, so it is no surprise that school taxes far outpace the tax revenue needed to run local government in most municipalities.

There was a time when teachers were underpaid. We made up for poor pay by giving them benefits beyond what private sector workers got. But NJ teachers now earn a comfortable living (for a job with 185 annual work days)[16] and are among the highest paid in the nation. Benefits have expanded as well.

Once, it was possible for school boards to negotiate with teacher unions and, if a contract wasn't reached in a reasonable time, impose its last best offer. That gave school boards power over unions, but it was a power rarely exercised. Schools boards are elected, and the public's oversight acted as a constraint. I doubt if this power was used more than a half-dozen times. But it was there as encouragement for *both* sides to negotiate fairly.

---

[16] Ramsey's teachers work 189 days per year, a concession that was gained and paid for by the BOE many years ago.

That is, it was there until the state legislature, under pressure from NJEA, removed it six years ago. Now, negotiations often drag on endlessly, with multiple fact-finding and mediation hoops a school board must jump through.

And while negotiations drag on, teachers use school children and their parents as pawns. In Ramsey, teachers took days off *en masse*, closing down schools when no holidays were scheduled. They refused to write college recommendation letters for high school seniors. They showed up at board meetings, causing trustees to walk a gantlet of placard-waving, slogan-chanting union militants and their supporters. These tactics were designed, of course, to pressure the school board to settle. Apparently, they worked.

When a state-appointed "fact finder" recommended a 16.95% pay raise over four years and *no* change in health insurance benefits, the Ramsey board abandoned its attempt to eliminate the costly "traditional" insurance plan it provides free for tenured teachers and their families and to substitute the less expensive "PPO" plan. It voted unanimously to adopt the report's recommendations as the "best deal it could get." Not surprisingly, Ramsey teachers voted a few days later to accept that sweetheart deal. All that remains are a few contract details to be worked out . . . and for Ramsey taxpayers to pick up the tab.

These union tactics happen so often throughout the state— Ridgewood teachers used them with equal success a few years back—they must be a page torn from NJEA's job action play book.

Our public employees and their unions simply do not want to face the economic realities of our time. I hold them and their leaders accountable for that, but I also fault elected officials in Trenton and I fault the voting (and non-voting) public. I blame our legislators and governor for their unconscionable conflicts of interest in accepting sizeable campaign contributions from public employee unions (Governor Corzine got $12,000 from NJEA for his inaugural festivities) and then enacting laws and regulations that give public employee unions their immense power over municipalities and school boards. And I blame us, the public, for letting that happen.

Attention Ramsey Property Tax Payers

You've read the newspaper reports of the deal recently concluded between the Board of Ed and the teachers union. After 20 months of often acrimonious negotiations, the Board capitulated, accepting a state fact-finder's *recommendation* that teachers get 16.95% in raises over four years and dropping its attempt to get modest health insurance concessions from the teachers.

The *average* Ramsey teacher's salary is $63,165. When this new contract expires in 2011, that average will be $74,571, and teachers will still have free health insurance, dental benefits, and an outstanding retirement pension. All based on 189 work days, or 38 work weeks, a year.

How many weeks do you work a year? Do you get free health insurance for your family? A pension that'll pay half your highest salary every year for the rest of your life? Lifetime health insurance benefits?

Tell me if you've had enough. If so, are you ready to do something about it? I don't mean just talk. Are you ready to work to change things, to take back control of the Ramsey public school system so we can get quality education at a reasonable cost? I am sick and tired of the teachers' union proclaiming that this exorbitant personnel cost is necessary to achieve a quality education. That is a self-serving declaration without merit. It is nonsense, especially in today's job market when there are likely 10 qualified applicants for every teaching position. St. Paul's Interparochial School and Don Bosco Prep provide their students with an excellent education, and they do it with a staff earning considerably less than Ramsey public school teachers—more than $10,000 a year less.

As my article above clearly shows, we cannot rely on state government to come to the rescue. That's not going to happen. We must take responsibility for our own future, and to achieve that, we need to put five new members on the Board of Ed—people who share our concerns and values. The deadline for filing 2009 election petitions is March 2nd, so time is of the essence. Let's meet to discuss our options. The *new* R.T.A. No, not the Ramsey Teachers Association. I'm talking about the *Ramsey Taxpayers Association.*

E-mail me or phone me to let me know of your willingness to participate. But if you volunteer, be prepared to work. We need people who will work the phones and stuff envelopes before school election day in April to get out the vote. You can be sure the teachers will be well organized to defeat us. We need highly qualified candidates to represent us. (Not me, please—I've done my duty.) It will take two years, but we can do it. And when 2011 rolls around and this newest contract expires, we can change direction for the good of our community. Yes, we can.

* * *

The Ramsey Teachers Association did not appreciate my butting in, to say the least. They responded with ads of their own and letters to the editor, mostly attacking me, personally. I was now invested fully in trying to right the course of the Ramsey Board of Education, as far as its approach to labor negotiations went. Despite my disinclination, I became one of eight candidates—three incumbents and five challengers—running in April 2009 for three seats on the board. My final self-paid article appeared in the local paper shortly after the election, the outcome of which provided me with one of the most memorable moments in my life. Here is that final article in this series, from the Ramsey Suburban News, April 29, 2009.

Thank you, Ramsey,

for your overwhelming support in the school board election last week.

- 3,348 of you went to the polls and voted. That turnout is astounding for an April school board election. It represents 33.5% of registered voters, but the registration figures are misleading because they are inflated with the names of folks who have moved or died. My father died in 2000, but is still listed as a registered voter in Ramsey (no, he didn't vote for me). Actual turnout was probably more like 40%, and I doubt if any municipality in Bergen County came close to that level.

- 1,940 of you voted for me and made me the top vote-getter, with more than 500 votes separating me and the next candidate. Almost six out of every 10 voters entering the booth cast their ballots for me, another astounding fact given that there were eight candidates for three seats. I don't think any candidate for Ramsey school board has ever received that many votes in a contested election.

What does it all mean? Well, in my mind this was support not for me personally, but for the views I put forth during my campaign. A clear mandate for change. It remains to be seen whether the current Board—eight of whom continue to serve, with me as the lone newcomer—will see things the same way. I have my doubts. Two indications lead me to believe it will be business as usual.

First, I had hoped to be assigned to the negotiations committee. After all, I did make this the main issue in my campaign and I was elected in a landslide. In addition, I have nine years experience negotiating contracts with public employee unions and led negotiations with Borough employees as mayor, getting significant health insurance concessions from them. I mean, it does seem logical that I would be able to do the most good for taxpayers on that committee, right? Wrong. I've been told that I will not be assigned to the negotiations committee because I have no choice in the matter and the other Board members would not like it. Business as usual.

Second, I requested that the Reorganization Meeting on April 30th be held in the high school auditorium to accommodate what I think might be a large turnout of residents who want to see me sworn in and who are hoping this will mark a new and balanced approach to public education, one that considers education excellence, of course, but also the cost and the public's ability to pay. But no. I've been told that the meeting on April 30th will take place at 7:30 p.m. in the 2nd-floor high school library, which will accommodate about 40 people comfortably and require folks to climb two flights of stairs. Business as usual.

Dear friends and fellow citizens of Ramsey, I've been up against such obstacles before. Rest assured—they do not daunt me. I shall engage my new colleagues on the Ramsey Board of Education in polite and reasoned discussion of the issues. I shall listen to their comments and opinions with respect and an open mind, with the hope they will do the same when I express my views. There will be one important exception to their business-as-usual rule. You will now have a voice on this school board. I shall do my best for you, for Ramsey, and for Ramsey's children.

/signed/ Richard Muti

Paid for by Richard Muti, Citizen of Ramsey

* * *

Postscript

I was sworn in as one of nine school trustees on the Ramsey Board of Education at the board's reorganization meeting on April 30, 2009, two days after the board had approved the four-year deal with the teachers' union—a hastily arranged approval, I think, because the board knew I might present some problems once I was an official member of that body.

It wasn't my intention to cause problems, but what I did intend to do was cause change in the board's attitude toward its fiscal responsibility to Ramsey's taxpayers and change in its labor negotiations. I saw right off, with eight of the "old" guard almost unanimously against me, that the road to change would be difficult. That fact was pointed out to me most emphatically when the board president, who would later become my ally on the board, refused to appoint me to the negotiations committee.

Eventually, I did gain a seat on the negotiations committee, which would become important as a new round of negotiations with the teachers' union loomed. The four-year deal the old board had agreed to, would actually expire on June 30, 2011, because of the length of the prior negotiations. And the whole process would begin again six months prior to that.

Things began to change on the board—attitudes and actions. Board members—some, not all—began to view me as a colleague and not as the enemy. I think they came to accept my sincerity, my strong desire for the Ramsey school system to succeed, and my love, albeit unrequited, for Ramsey's teachers.

Throughout my public career, I've continually praised my Ramsey public school teachers as being the second most important influence in my life, after my parents. I wanted them to be compensated well, but I also insisted that they recognize the new economic realities we were being forced to deal with.

In 2010, another new, cost-conscious board member was elected. In 2011, still another. In 2012, I ran for re-election and was, once again, the top vote-getter, but more important, two new board members were elected with me, both of whom I had supported. There were now five new Ramsey BOE trustees, enough to command a majority of the board. And, while there were differences among us, we all held similar views, I believe, on the need to control costs. Moreover, several of the old board members still remaining also began to support me on a number of issues I brought to the forefront.

While preparing for the new round of negotiations, I discovered that there were four married couples in the school district with both spouses receiving separate health insurance policies, in contravention of New Jersey law. What's more, this policy of providing duplicative benefits for both spouses had been going on for 20 years and had probably wasted more than $1 million in taxpayer money. I wrote a legal brief on the matter, submitted it to fellow board members, and asked them to verify my findings with our board attorney. That happened, and, when the board attorney validated my legal analysis, the board voted to end the policy of providing duplicative benefits in our district, thereby saving about $65,000 a year. It was the first of a number of successes.

In my research, I also discovered a New Jersey law, and New Jersey Supreme Court decision, that limited a school board's approval authority regarding teacher salary policy to a maximum of three years. That is, a board could obligate itself and future boards to one, two, or three years of teacher salary policies, but no more than that. It appeared to me that the four-year deal the board had approved two days before I was sworn in violated that New Jersey law. Once again, I wrote a legal brief, submitted it to my colleagues, and asked them to have the board attorney review the matter. And, once again, the board attorney agreed with my legal analysis. After the board directed our attorney to file an objection to that fourth year of salary policy, the New Jersey Commissioner of Education ruled, on October 21, 2011, that the fourth year did, indeed, violate state law and was "null and void."

The RTA appealed. In November 2012, the Appellate Division upheld the Commissioner's decision to void the fourth year of the teachers' contract. The RTA is now seeking review by the N.J. Supreme Court.

The most important legacy of my first school board election victory in April 2009 was achieved on September 20, 2012, when the board unanimously approved a new teacher contract, which I had an important role in negotiating. For the first time in 14 years, there would be health insurance concessions made by the Ramsey Teachers Association— significant concessions that would save borough taxpayers close to a million a year over the cost of the old insurance plans that had been in place for so long. It was a victory achieved by concerted, purposeful board action, not by me, alone. But I won't be shy about claiming my share of credit as the catalyst.

Chapter 28

I come from a family of police officers: an uncle, four cousins, two nephews. This article—a featured piece in The Record on Sunday, February 8, 2009—caused a bit of upset, especially with one cousin who had been president of his local police union. But I learned a long time ago, at my father's side when he was involved in politics, that yes, we are fiercely loyal to family, but our duty to the public, when we hold public office, comes first. From my time as the chief administrator of the Bergen County Prosecutor's Office and continuing through my service as mayor of Ramsey and as a school trustee, I've been a strong supporter of public employees, but in a measured way that also takes into consideration the burden on taxpayers. As with everything else in life, a balance must be struck between competing interests.

Should Towns Rein In Police Pay?

Public employee unions have a chokehold on municipal budgets, but local governments should not look to Trenton to solve the problem. Trenton *is* the problem.

The recent decision by a state arbitrator to award Closter police a 16 percent pay raise, despite that town's financial woes, is a case in point. Don't blame the arbitrator. He was just following laws handed down by the most union-friendly legislature in the nation. Because public employees do not have the right to strike, the State has decreed they must be protected from local officials.

Police were given the power to reject any contract offer and take their municipal employers to binding arbitration. But the rules established by the legislature are so stacked in favor of police that many municipalities give in to union demands rather than risk a budget-busting arbitrator's award. This creates a cycle of police raises that just keeps building, because one criterion arbitrators must weigh is what raises and benefits other towns in the region give *their* police.

Most police officers in so-called affluent suburbs routinely reach six-figure incomes (including overtime) after just six or eight years on the job. Their other perks—liberal vacation, sick and personal days, free family health insurance, longevity bonuses, uniform allowances, and a pension plan that lets them retire after 25 years at three-quarters pay and health insurance for life—seem crafted not for public employees, but for NY Yankee free agents.

For each police officer in your town, think $3,000,000. That's how much taxpayers will pay out over an officer's career. Yes, police take risks and deserve something extra, but balance is needed. New York City police, just as dedicated and arguably facing more danger, earn about two thirds of what their counterparts in most New Jersey suburban towns earn.

What are mayors and councils to do, then, on behalf of their taxpaying citizens to achieve a square deal with police unions, even when faced with the stacked deck Trenton politicians have handed them?

Police unions are the hardest to deal with because of binding arbitration. They know they have that hammer, and if your union negotiating committee is an unreasonable bunch, they will not hesitate to beat you about the head with it—especially when they are represented by one of the gunslinger lawyers who specialize in this type of litigation.

As mayor of Ramsey in 2003, I took charge of negotiations with our police department, whose contract expired the day I took office. Fortunately, I had responsible union negotiators I could deal with. There was some back and forth, of course. Each side had to test the resolve and mettle of the other. But we were able to reach a settlement within 10 months, a short time frame as police negotiations go. Here was the key to our success.

We looked for and found a *win-win* scenario, a strategy whereby each side could get something it desperately needed. The police wanted enhanced retirement health insurance. I wanted to change their health insurance from the most expensive "traditional" plan to a more reasonably priced "PPO" plan. And I wanted to keep pay raises at or below the rate of inflation.

We both achieved our goals. The police won the ability to retire at 25 years with full health benefits (formerly, they had to serve 30 years to get that). That helped them, but in a way it also helped taxpayers, because we were able to replace higher cost officers sooner, with less expensive new hires. I got the PPO insurance plan I wanted and the lowest pay raise of any negotiated police contract in the state. As a result, Ramsey property tax payers saved $120,000 a year, each and every year going forward.

But what can you do if you are faced with unreasonable employee unions? As chief administrator of the Bergen County Prosecutor's Office in the late 1990s, I had the responsibility of negotiating all labor contracts. We were able to settle with two of our police unions, but the third filed for binding arbitration.

When faced with a situation like that, toughness matters. You must thoroughly prepare for battle and have the best professional help on your side. I represented the county at the hearing and wrote the legal briefs. Many of these officers were my friends, but I was ruthless in my cross examination of them and in my defense of county taxpayers. That is the only way to win an arbitration case with police unions.

And win we did. The arbitrator's award favored the county in almost all points of contention, but most especially in the size of the raises given—raises lower than those I had offered before arbitration.

A municipality facing a police union fight can and should take measures to protect its taxpayers. Given the uncertainty of arbitrators' awards, a freeze on police hiring should be considered, as well as a moratorium on promotions. You cannot take on new officers or promote officers when you don't know the financial impact. Local government owes its citizens strong police protection, but it must be protection they can afford. State aid to municipalities will be cut even more drastically in the future. If police departments are the most expensive part of any municipal budget, that is the place to start controlling costs.

Chapter 29

Newly elected New Jersey Governor Chris Christie took office in January 2010. In this featured article in The Record, on Sunday, February 7, 2010, I give the new governor some advice. I don't know if he saw the article, but one of my recommendations was adopted within a few months. It advocated elimination of duplicative health insurance coverage for public employees and, as far as I know, had not been publicly discussed before I raised the issue in this article. It would become an important cost-saver for all New Jersey taxpayers.

A Teachable Moment

Scott Brown's victory in Massachusetts may be the "I'm-mad-as-hell-and-I'm-not-going-to-take-it-anymore" new reality of American politics, but Chris Christie's victory in blue-state New Jersey was the harbinger.

Christie's election set Democrats back on their heels. During his inaugural address, when he called on Assembly Speaker Sheila Oliver and Senate Majority Leader Stephen Sweeney to join hands in a symbolic gesture of bi-partisanship, the new governor scored a political master stroke. To their credit, Democrats appear willing to work with Christie. Sen. Sweeney, a union leader in real life, has already signed on to pension reform. Maybe sanity is returning to Trenton.

The biggest loser in the election was the New Jersey Education Association (NJEA), the statewide teachers' union. NJEA is used to being the 800-pound gorilla in any political fight, but candidate Chris Christie didn't even seek their endorsement. He took it as a given they would back his rival, and, indeed, they went "all-in" for Corzine.

Having smashed the aura of NJEA invincibility, Governor Christie has an opening to do something really spectacular with New Jersey's teachers. But to achieve that goal, he needs to tone down the rhetoric and engage in serious discussions with NJEA leaders. He needs to unclench his iron fist just enough to hold in it the olive branch of reasonable compromise. Teacher contracts are decided at the district level, but NJEA has influence. If the powerful union agrees to a compromise with the governor, it can get that deal accepted locally.

Teachers are not the enemy. They are valued members of society, for they hold our future in their professional grasp every working day. They should be well compensated, but that compensation must also fit economic circumstances. Teachers have been getting four to five percent pay raises, on average, and their benefits packages are far too generous. That's not fair to taxpayers, especially now.

With school taxes comprising 60-70 percent of every property tax dollar and with personnel costs—salaries and benefits—consuming 70-80 percent of every school budget, bringing personnel costs under control is the irrefutable key to property tax *gradualism*. I say "gradualism" because property taxes are never going down. Small increases would be a triumph.

Here are five things the governor can do to rein in costs—something for teachers, something for taxpayers.

1. Merit-based pay is a nice idea, but basing it on standardized test results has drawbacks. For example, children with learning problems are often assigned to the best teachers. Improved test results for those students might be relatively modest, but the teaching talent to achieve those results might have been extraordinary. Also, how does one remove favoritism in merit pay decisions? NJEA is opposed to merit pay. Take it off the table for five years and establish a commission (unpaid volunteers from different interest groups) to devise a workable merit pay plan. In return, get a more realistic process to rid schools of clearly incompetent teachers. Overcoming tenure to remove a really bad teacher is time-consuming and expensive for local districts, so much so that few even attempt it.

2. Bring fiscal health back to the teachers' pension system. Come up with a plan to fully fund that program within 10 years, and stick to it. Teachers have been making their pension contributions. It's the government that has robbed Peter to pay Paul. Well, Peter is sick and tired of that kind of fiscal mismanagement.

3. Eliminate "double-dipping" on health insurance benefits. Right now, a teacher may be employed in one school district and her spouse in the same district or in another district or other public job. Under current law, both marriage partners can demand health insurance with full family benefits to be paid for by their respective public employers. Why are we permitting this, when one family insurance package is all that is needed? No public employee should be getting a wasteful duplication of this very expensive benefit.

4. Create a two-tiered health insurance system that is standard for the entire state—one for teachers new to the job and one for those who have tenure. There are aspects of today's public sector health insurance that are expensive relics of another time. For example, the "traditional" health insurance plan must be eliminated from public employee contracts and more reasonably priced plans (like PPO's, POS's, and HMO's) substituted.

5. I don't agree with freezing salaries in contravention of existing contracts, but give school districts a level playing field for future negotiations. In 2003, the legislature ended a school district's right to impose its "last best offer" after negotiations fail to reach a settlement. This unilateral right had rarely been invoked, but it motivated unions to bargain in good faith. When that provision was struck in 2003, unions gained the upper hand. Thereafter, contract talks often dragged on, and costs escalated.

Teachers realize change is inevitable. I think they're fearful Governor Christie will overcorrect, casting them as scapegoats. Union leaders sense this angst, but I also think they're ready to accept a fair deal, for the good of their members and the public they serve.

Chapter 30

Like many Americans and public officials—President Barack Obama among them—I have evolved in my attitude toward our LGBT fellow citizens. I've always been in favor of equal rights, but I've come to see how that is not enough. Here is my "In the Arena" blog post from January 9, 2010.

Forsaking the Golden Rule

I wonder if religious groups opposed marriage between whites and blacks during the era of miscegenation laws—lasting through the mid-20th Century in some state bastions of bigotry—as vehemently as they do the marriage of gays or lesbians. Did they liken the marriage of a white person and a black person to the coupling of a human and an animal? Did they go on and on about the "sanctity" of marriage or the long-standing tradition that only members of the same race should marry, all the while ignoring the prevalence of divorce, abandonment, and dysfunction in those same sacred, traditional unions? Did they forget their scripture, then as now, and pay no heed to the teachings of Matthew and Luke that, in everything, we should do to others what we would have them do to us. That we should, in effect, live . . . and let live.

In the latest affront to justice and equal rights for the gay and lesbian community, the New Jersey State Senate last week defeated the Marriage Equality Act by a vote of 20 to 14. The proposed law would have ended the sham of "civil union" or "domestic partnership" equality and would have elevated New Jersey into the company of five other progressive states (Massachusetts, Connecticut, Vermont, New Hampshire, and Iowa) who recognize the time has come to right a grievous wrong.

In a telling front-page photo in Friday's *Record*, under the headline "Gay Marriage Loses," the pain of the moment is written on the faces of gay and lesbian couples sitting in the senate gallery and anxiously tracking each vote, as they await their inevitable fate, given the New Jersey legislature's history of cowardice and political gamesmanship.

These are the faces of our sons and daughters, our nieces and nephews, our cousins, uncles and aunts . . . and our fellow citizens and Americans—all of them entitled to, but not getting, the same equal protection under our laws and Constitution the rest of us enjoy.

When I ran for state senate in the 39th legislative district in 2003, I came out for civil unions, but not gay and lesbian marriage. I was wrong. And the New Jersey state senators who privately assured the gay and lesbian community of their support for years, but who lacked the courage last Thursday to stand up in public and give that support are wrong.

Sen. Loretta Weinberg, the feisty Bergen County Democrat who stood up to political boss Joe Ferriero, urged senators to find their backbone and do what is right—support the bill she co-sponsored.

"To my colleagues who are wavering, do what your conscience tells you to do," she said. "Vote yes."

Alas, there were few profiles in courage when the tally was completed at 4:40 p.m. I must say the most courageous "yes" vote came from Sen. Bill Baroni of Mercer County, the only Republican to support the measure. Sen. Baroni has been impressive throughout his brief legislative career, in both the NJ state assembly and, now, the senate. He is young, and I fervently hope I live to see the day when he becomes governor of this ethically-challenged state. Sen. Bob Gordon of Bergen, a Democrat, is another shining example of the right kind of politician, the kind we so sorely lack in this state.

There were also a few prime examples of the rank cowardice and slimy politics that permeate our state house and halls of government. Sen. Paul Sarlo, a triple-dipper at the public trough (state senator, mayor of Wood-Ridge, and municipal engineer) and facilitator of special interest legislation to benefit his construction industry friends, abstained from voting altogether. Sarlo said he was "just not prepared to support it," but, evidently, did not want his opposition recorded in a vote.

Another egregious performance came from the soon-to-be senate president, Democrat Stephen Sweeney of Gloucester County, who recently ousted long-time senate president Richard Codey with the help of party bosses in South Jersey and Newark. Sweeney also abstained from voting, but said he was in favor of the measure. Unbelievable, especially coming from someone who will be the senate leader in a few days. Sweeney said he did not vote "yes" because more Republicans did not vote yes, and he did not want to give Republicans a campaign issue next year, when the entire state legislature is up for reelection.

There's an interesting thought. A pipe dream, but interesting. What if half of these calcified, artery-hardened, closed-minded representatives of ours were handed their pink slips by New Jersey voters in November

2011? What if we had a few dozen more Baronis and Weinbergs and Gordons and others with fresh faces and fresh ideas and courage. Just a little courage, to take over our state institutions of government and begin the long, difficult process of simply doing the right thing—not only in socially responsible matters like the Marriage Equality Act, but also in fiscally responsible matters like the future viability and financial well-being of our state.

Like I said, a pipe dream.

Chapter 31

This short blog post—"In the Arena," October 30, 2010—shows my on-going contempt for the lack of political backbone in most elected officials. The title comes from a noted criminal case in which a disturbed serial killer scrawled this message at each murder scene: "Stop me before I kill again."

Here, the New Jersey State Legislature put a question on our ballot that sought a voter sanction to prevent them, in the future, from misappropriating funds collected for a specific purpose.

"Stop Me Before I Steal Again"

The one public question on the ballot this coming Tuesday is whether or not New Jersey should set aside in a separate fund the unemployment benefit taxes taken from your check each payday to pay . . . well, to pay unemployment benefits. You see, it turns out Trenton lawmakers (we should be calling them Trenton *lawbreakers*) have been taking that money and using it for other things, like funding the ever-growing operating expenses of state government. They diverted billions of dollars over the years. It was an easy way to pay for things—a hidden way that no one would notice, like they'd notice higher taxes or increased borrowing against tobacco trust funds (they did that, too) and transportation trust funds (they did that, too) and other "trust" funds.

This raiding of the unemployment money came to light during the current recession, when record numbers of New Jerseyans found themselves in need of the money that had supposedly been set aside for them. That's the whole idea behind set-asides—you collect it in good times, so it can be available in bad times, like a rainy day fund. The money wasn't there, of course, and the poor souls who needed it were in danger of not having it. Ultimately, the state borrowed enough from the federal government (good old Uncle Sam, a friend when we need him, a punching bag when we don't) to make the payments, at least so far. Now, the folks in Trenton say we need a constitutional amendment to prevent future Trenton lawbreakers from doing the same thing—stealing unemployment tax money to pay for other things.

It's the same old story. Politicians taking the easy way out so they can continue their posturing, their sloganeering, and their 15-second sound bites, with as much bluster and self-assuredness as they can muster. Just once I'd like one of them to exhibit thoughtful consideration and substance on any important issue, rather than the outright certainty and pat answers they have for everything. Unfortunately, I don't see that happening.

I urge everyone to vote *Yes* on this public question this Tuesday. We do need to stop them before they steal again.

Chapter 32

In this essay from The Record, Sunday, December 18, 2011, I support a provision of most public employee contracts, but for the reason that it also benefits taxpayers. In all my negotiations with public employee unions, I've strived to find win-win solutions to the problems we faced.

An Rx for Sick Pay[17]

A Doctor is Needed, Not an Undertaker

One public employee benefit in the news lately is sick leave payouts—the money a worker gets when cashing in accumulated unused sick leave at retirement. Gov. Christie has taken up the cause, citing exorbitant payouts and urging legislative action to eliminate this common feature of public employee contracts. Newspapers, including *The Record*, have joined the public clamor for change.

The sick leave payout issue is not as clear-cut as Gov. Christie and others assert. Yes, such payouts have been abused, primarily because elected officials haven't done a better job of containing them. With proper controls, encouraging workers *not* to take sick leave is good public policy . . . but the horror stories still abound.

I became mayor of Ramsey, my hometown, in 2003, soundly defeating a four-term, 16-year incumbent. One of the issues that insured my victory was a bloated compensation package the borough was paying its part-time borough attorney—over $250,000 a year in pay and benefits, far surpassing what many larger municipalities in New Jersey were paying their legal counsel. I was able to *encourage* this attorney to retire, but was aghast when I had to hand him, because of borough personnel policies, a going-away present of more than $100,000—mostly payment for his unused sick leave.

During my tenure as mayor, I took steps to prevent this from happening again. The borough council and I instituted a cap on such payouts for all but the police union. There, we had bigger cost factors to deal with, like getting rid of the expensive traditional health insurance plan. With binding arbitration mandated for police and state arbitrators biased toward unions, municipalities couldn't attempt too big a bite of the cost-control apple all at once. A cap on sick leave had to wait.

Sick leave is supposed to be used for actual work-preventing illness. If an employee's sick leave goes beyond a few days, public employers can demand an independent medical opinion to prevent abuse; but no local government has the resources or the will to check up on every worker who takes a sick day here and there for an undisclosed ailment.

What happens when a public employee takes a sick day? In schools, the superintendent must call in a substitute teacher, thereby necessitating payment not only to that substitute but also to the teacher home on paid sick leave. In municipalities, another employee may have to be called in on overtime (at time-and-a-half or double-time) to replace the worker home on sick leave. In other words, an employee taking sick days often doubles the cost to taxpayers. So, how do we control it? We could institute onerous measures to oversee the taking of sick leave, but why establish intrusive new policies when a reasonable "come-to-work" incentive can accomplish the same goal?

Right now, there is a $15,000 cap on sick leave payouts for most state workers and school employees. Some towns, like Ramsey, have capped their workers' payouts. Providing an incentive for public employees to hold on to their sick leave is a good idea. It gives them an income cushion, should they become ill, and a modest nest egg at the end of a long career of public service. It is also cost effective for taxpayers.

We need to make a cap on sick leave payouts universal, whether the figure is $15,000 or $10,000, but make it harder to reach that level, perhaps by giving a half-day pay credit for each unused sick day in a retiring employee's "bank." Also, instead of paying out for unused sick days using the rate of pay at retirement, use a mid-career earning rate so that sick leave banked at the entry level does not become a bonanza later, when pay has doubled or tripled.

The anger over public employee salaries and benefits is understandable. These workers used to earn salaries much lower than their private sector counterparts; towns and school districts made up for that monetary shortfall by fattening the benefits side of compensation packages. But then, thanks primarily to the political clout of public employee unions, state legislators—collective beneficiaries of millions in union campaign contributions and either targets or beneficiaries of massive union get-out-the-vote efforts, depending on how they voted—enacted laws that made it much harder to control personnel costs at the local level.

The result, achieved slowly over the last decade or so, was that public employee salaries increased dramatically, surpassing in many instances the salaries earned by non-public workers with similar education and skills. And, while salaries shot up, public workers' benefits stayed as lucrative as they had been during the low-salary era. Now, at a time when the private sector is hurting badly and health insurance costs are skyrocketing, local property taxpayers, many of whom are unemployed for the first time in their lives, are shocked and sometimes angry at the compensation packages of public workers, including the iron-clad job security those workers take for granted. And taxpayers want something done about it.

Gov. Christie has accomplished a number of good things lately, like the pension and insurance benefits reform law enacted last June. It will save municipalities, collectively, hundreds of millions in the long term. But the public policy problems we face rarely lend themselves to pat answers and one-size-fits-all solutions. The sick leave payout issue is a case in point. Leaders who are absolutely sure they are right about everything make me nervous.

Chapter 33

Once again, I got a featured spot in The Record's Opinion section, on Sunday, January 8, 2012, to speak to an important public policy issue— the right of local property taxpayers to vote on school budgets, the most costly element of their tax bills. The Ramsey school board supported my position and voted to keep our school budget and trustee elections in April so that citizens would also have a say on the budget.

Losing a Say on School Budgets[18]

The public's right to vote on school budgets—the most costly component of property taxes in New Jersey—is about to be extinguished, thanks to an unholy alliance of special interests and the state legislature.

A few legislators have tried for years to move school voting, for both board candidates and budgets, to the regular November election cycle, when higher voter turnouts are more likely. Normal school voting has been in late April, the theory being that a six-month separation from the partisanship in November would insulate schools from political influence.

That noble sentiment was the justification the New Jersey Education Association (NJEA) and New Jersey School Boards Association (NJSBA) used for their past opposition to moving the school vote. In reality, both organizations preferred the low-voter turnout of April to the higher-voter turnout of November for one simple reason: It gave them a better chance to control the result.

NJEA and NJSBA have one overriding common interest, despite all the haggling and bickering over labor issues. Both abhor school budget defeats and both work hard to ensure school budget passage. Personnel costs—salaries and benefits—make up 70-80 percent of most school budgets. A budget defeat means the local mayor and council will make cuts, their legal right. They don't have to cut, but they almost always do. Cuts affect both labor and management in a school district through smaller pay increases, if not layoffs, less money for maintenance, program elimination, and other measures.

When turnout is low, as in April, get-out-the-vote efforts can usually—not always but usually—overpower any opposition by frustrated taxpayers, especially those with no children in school. Typically, teachers volunteer to make calls to parents the night before an election to remind them to vote. PTOs urge their members to vote. Administrators send emails out and notes home in backpacks with the same message. It's illegal to use public resources to encourage a "Yes" vote on the budget, but there is no prohibition against promoting voter turnout among the group most likely to vote "Yes"—parents of school children.

With April turnout in the low 20 percent range and with parents of school children likely to represent two-thirds of the electorate, one can see the allure of April voting to NJEA and NJSBA. Yet, both organizations have now joined to give their blessing to this proposed new law moving school voting to November. Why? Because the proposed law also provides a mechanism to take away from the public the right to vote on school budgets.

There is a two percent cap on the amount a school district can raise the property tax levy. Under this new law, so long as a school district's proposed budget is within the two percent cap, taxpayers may very well lose their vote on it. The legislature and governor have bought NJEA and NJSBA approval for the move to November voting by taking away the public's right to approve the most significant aspect of local property taxes—about 65 percent of the tax bill.

Some will say there's no need for a vote if the district stays within the two percent cap, but who is to judge that a two percent increase in school taxes means the district is automatically doing a good job? Shouldn't that be the province of taxpayers footing the bill? School boards are still answerable to the electorate by standing for reelection, but it takes time to change the composition of a school board. With only a third up for reelection at any one time, it would take years to gain a majority on nine-member boards. The public should have a more immediate way to express not only its displeasure with a board's stewardship, but also its assent.

The new law has a local option regarding November voting and termination of budget voting rights, accomplished in one of three ways. The school board, by a majority vote, can move the elections and end voting on the budget, provided it stays within the two percent cap. Or, the municipal governing body can act in the same way. Finally, 15 percent of those who voted in the last presidential election can petition to have the measure put on the ballot for the public to consider. Any one of these methods will accomplish the same result—November voting for school board candidates and no voting on school budgets that keep within the two percent cap.

Proponents also point to cost savings by eliminating April elections, a spurious argument. The Office of Legislative Services, non-partisan arm of the state legislature, citing evidence that districts spend an average .08 percent of their budgets to pay for April voting (a miniscule *eight one-hundredths of one percent*), concluded, "There will be no fiscal impact in a school district that does not change the date of its annual school elections." Moreover, any savings would likely evaporate when the municipality assesses the school district for its share of the costs incurred for dual-purposed November voting. By the way, Ramsey spent about three one-hundredths of one percent on its last April election.

Direct democracy—the ability of citizens to participate first-hand in decisions that affect them—is rare in America. It exists in town-hall meetings in some New England states and in public voting on initiatives and referenda in some states. And it exists in the time-honored tradition of New Jersey citizens exercising their right to say "Yes" or "No" to school budgets. Public officials who act to extinguish that right should be ashamed of themselves.

Seventeen-year-old Rosaria Potenza (right), with her younger
sister, shortly after their arrival at Ellis Island on March 17, 1907.
The girls had emigrated from Acri, in Calabria, Italy. Rosaria
would wed Sergio Muti in 1909 or 1910 and have nine children,
including the author's father, Mauro Richard Muti.

The growing Muti family, c. 1920, on the back steps of a rented home in Ramsey, before Sergio would build "the house on Carol Street." Mauro Richard stands behind his mother. The other children, clockwise, are Carmella (Minnie), Angelina (Sally), Josephine (Josie), and Vincent. Four more children to come.

Rosaria, around 1925 or 1926, with eight of her children, dressed in their Sunday best. The children, left to right, are Nick, Mauro, Josie, Vincent, Minnie (partially hidden), Sally, Anthony, and Rosie.

The family, dressed up for a special occasion, around 1926 or 1927: Sergio, Minnie, Mauro, Sally, Vince, Josie, Nick, Rosie, Tony, and Rosaria. They did not own the car.

Sergio Muti (right), with older brother Nicolo Muti, standing in front of the gray-stuccoed house on Carol Street in June 1927, one year before Sergio's death from a work accident.

The Muti siblings, in 1927 or 1928. The older children, from right to left:
Minnie, Mauro, Sally, Vince, Josie, and Nick, who is trying to settle down
a rambunctious Tony. Vince has his arm on Rosie, in front of him. Jean, the
youngest of the nine children, is not shown. She would be born in late 1928,
after the death of her father, Sergio.

Mauro Richard Muti, at 17, in his yearbook photo, Ramsey High School, Class of 1930.

Left: Mauro Richard, in the mid-1930s, on his favorite mode of transportation at the time. Right: "Dick" Muti, with his own Model-T, mid- to late-1930's.

The four brothers--Vince, Tony, Dick, and Nick (left to right)--in front of their home, in 1938 or 1939.

Mafalda Stella Muti ("Muffie"), on her wedding day in April 1939. Her gown would be worn by a younger sister, before being shipped to Italy for further use.

Muffie and Dick at the beach in the summer of 1939.

The Community Lunch at 45 E. Main St., Ramsey. Muffie and Dick operated the luncheonette from 1939 to 1955. In 1956, they opened Milano Restaurant, named for Muffie's family and destined to make full use of her cooking skills, learned at the side of her mother, Pia Milano. Varka Restaurant now occupies the site on Spruce Street, Ramsey.

Vince Muti working the soda fountain at Community Lunch, in 1939 or 1940.

The Community Lunch, during World War II.

The author, at left, in 1941 in front of the house on Carol Street with his cousin Sonny, Minnie's only child. With both parents working, the author spent most of his childhood in that house, cared for by his paternal grandmother, Rosaria. One of the essays in this book, aptly titled, "The House on Carol Street," recalls those years.

Sgt. Vince Muti, U.S. Army Air Corps, Dick Muti, Petty Officer 2nd Class Nick Muti, U.S. Navy.

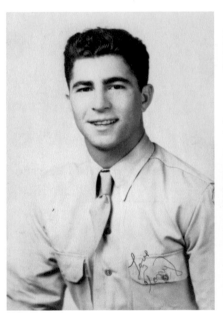

Left: Tony Muti, who left high school to join the army in 1944. He fought with Patton's Third Army across northern France into Germany and was decorated by the United States and French governments. Right: Nick Muti during the war, with sisters Rosie, Minnie, Josie, and Sally (left to right).

Sgt. Vince Muti, or could it be David Niven?

Sgt. Vince Muti, standing beneath his tailgunner post in the B-24 Liberator. He flew more than 20 missions over France and Germany before being wounded by shrapnel.

Left: Vince Muti spent six months in British hospitals recuperating from his wounds. He was awarded the Purple Heart and multiple Air Medals with Oak Leaf clusters. He returned from the war and had a long career as a letter carrier with the U.S. Post Office. Right: Rosaria ("Rose") Muti, in 1944.

Rose Muti clutching the four-year-old author at his birthday party in June 1944. Rose holds the author's one-year old sister, Rosemarie. Cousins Carmella Rittendale, Barbara Scafuro, Vincent Muti, and Sonny Berkhout (left to right) share the occasion.

Nick Muti, the sharpest dresser in the family, in the late 1940's. His argyle socks were probably hand-knitted for him by one of his sisters.

Dick Muti in the late 1940's in his fireman's uniform. He would serve in the Ramsey Volunteer Fire Department as an active and exempt member for 63 years.

The author, 10, with sister Rita, 4, and sister Rosemarie, 7, on the occasion of Rosemarie's First Holy Communion in 1950.

Dick Muti, behind the counter of his luncheonette, in the early 1950's.

Hugo Milano, Muffie Muti's younger brother, married Jean Marie Muti, Dick Muti's youngest sister, on September 14, 1952. This wedding day photo captures all nine Muti siblings with their mother and spouses. The couples, left to right, are Larry and Josie Scafuro, Dick and Muffie Muti (he gave the bride away), Vince and Dorothy Muti, Eddie and Minnie Berkhout, Hugo and Jean Milano, Sally Muti standing behind her mother Rosaria Muti, Ernie and Rose Rittendale, Tony and Vickie Muti, and Nick and Gloria Muti.

Left: Ramsey Chamber of Commerce president Dick Muti and VFW member Jack Graham, raising Old Glory in the early 1950's. The Chamber and the VFW joined together to install flags in front of every business on Main Street. Merchants flew the flags on holidays and other important occasions. (Photo by C. Trevelyan.)

Below: VFW member Jack Graham unfurls the flag in front of the Community Lunch, which advertises "home cooking" and "Italian American style blue plate dinners." (Photo by C. Trevelyan.)

M. Richard Muti (third from left) taking the oath as a Ramsey councilman for the first time, in January 1955, shortly before his 42nd birthday. He would go on to serve nine years--five as council president--before being elected Tax Assessor for the Borough of Ramsey, a post he would hold for 30 years, until his retirement in 1993 at age 80. Also taking the oath in this picture are Councilman Roy Forsberg (left), Mayor Alexander Eichorn (second from left) and Councilman Jack Adams (hidden). Borough Attorney James Muth (fourth from left) administers the oath to all four newly elected officials. (Photo courtesy of The Dater Archives.)

Dick Muti and his friend and fellow Ramsey businessman, Ed Syder, on the Community Lunch's last day, July 29, 1955. Dick holds a sign announcing the new restaurant he and Muffie would open less than a year later.

The author and his father, in 1955 or 1956.

Dick Muti and his brother Nick, who came on board to run the cocktail lounge at Milano Restaurant in 1957.

Borough Attorney James Muth (second from left) swears in newly re-elected Councilman M. Richard Muti for his second three-year term in January 1958, along with newly elected Councilwoman Adele Kelly, as Mayor John Elliot (left) looks on. Elliot, representing the entrenched Republican establishment, would clash frequently with Muti over their different approaches to governing. Muti, also a Republican, favored a more progressive, reform-minded party. The rupture would be complete when, in early 1960, Muti resigned from the Republican Club, where he had served as president, and entered the spring primary election as an Independent Republican council candidate. Calling Muti a "game political battler," The Ramsey Journal characterized the upcoming primary contest as a chance for voters to show "whether they would like to see more of Mr. Muti's methods of dealing with municipal problems, or are willing to let the Republican Club representatives take complete charge of municipal affairs."

Left: The only formal portrait of M. Richard Muti, other than his high school yearbook picture, probably from the late 1950's.

Below: Former Ramsey mayor Al Eichorn, still a Republican Club stalwart, lights a symbolic, congratulatory cigar for Councilman M. Richard Muti in the late 1950's, after Muti-backed Independent Republican Alton Zabriskie, a local drugstore owner, defeated the organization's council candidate in a special election. (Photo courtesy of The Dater Archives.)

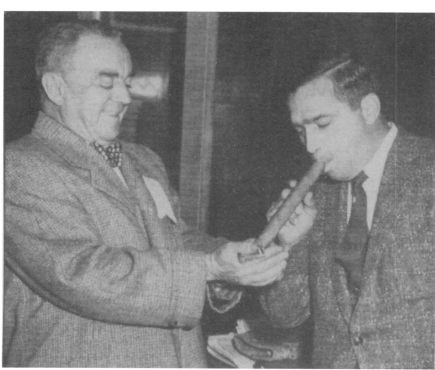

Rose Muti and her children celebrate her 70th birthday in 1959 at Milano Restaurant. Standing, left to right, Tony, Dick, Vince, and Nick. Seated, left to right, Jean, Josie, Minnie, Rose, Sally, and Rosie.

Midshipman 4th Class Richard Muti with his parents in the dining room of Milano Restuarant, while home from Annapolis on Christmas leave in 1960.

At the January 1961 Reorganization Meeting, Borough Attorney James Muth
(left) swears in newly elected Democratic Mayor Paul Huot, Council President
M. Richard Muti, Councilman Henry Carlson, and Councilman Tom Waldron
(left to right). Mayor Huot, whose wife Patricia would be elected to the council
in the future, served one term and later was appointed to the Superior Court of
New Jersey, where he had a long and distinguished career. In January 2003,
when author Richard Muti would himself be sworn in as the newly elected
Democratic mayor of Ramsey, retired Judge Paul Huot, his friend and mentor,
would administer the oath. (Photo courtesy of The Dater Archives.)

M. Richard Muti,
Ramsey's tax assessor,
endorses Emil Porfido,
a local businessman
and Democratic candi-
date for mayor in 1974.
Porfido would win a
razor-thin victory that
November, but would
go on to serve 12 years
as one of Ramsey's
most popular mayors.
Porfido returned the
favor 28 years later,
when he endorsed the
author in his successful
mayoral bid, unseating
a four-term Republican
incumbent.

Above: M. Richard Muti holding his first grandchild, Jeffrey Sergio Muti, in March 1965, in Milton, Florida, where the author was undergoing flight training.

Below: Dick Muti with his mother, Rose Muti, in the late 1960's. Rose Muti died in April 1970 at age 80.

The author and his father share a moment together to go over paperwork, probably in the early 1980's.

The author, marching in Ramsey's centennial parade in September 2008, behind a banner honoring his service as mayor of his hometown, 2003-2006. Defeated for re-election by a narrow margin in November 2006, the author would later serve his community further as a trustee on the Ramsey Board of Education.

Chapter 34

Changing the way New Jersey school boards structure teacher contracts, so as to require boards to follow the law and not grant teachers more than three years of salary guides, was an important accomplishment during my service on the Ramsey Board of Education. This article, published in the January-February 2012 edition of School Leader, the bi-monthly magazine of the New Jersey School Boards Association, gave school trustees throughout the state an explanation of the issue and the reasons for my advocacy in favor of compliance.

Most school boards, I'm afraid, were willing to ignore the law for the sake of convenience. If they granted more than three years of salary guides, they wouldn't have to undertake the difficult process of negotiations so often. The problem with that, besides being illegal, is that it commits school boards to significant expenditures—salaries and benefits are always the lion's share of their budgets—too far into the future, when economic conditions may very well have changed for the worse.

The Ramsey Teachers Association appealed this decision by the New Jersey Commissioner of Education in favor of the Ramsey school board, but on November 21, 2012, the Appellate Division of the Superior Court upheld the Ramsey board and the Commissioner, using language almost identical to my original legal brief, the spark that ignited this whole controversy.

The Death of 2+2 (and 1+3)

When school boards and teacher unions conclude protracted and sometimes acrimonious negotiations a year or two beyond an old contract's expiration, neither side wants to repeat that debilitating process too soon. And so, the parties often agree to expanded settlements—either a 2+2 deal or a 1+3 deal—that allow a breather before negotiations begin anew. They structure the settlement to provide two years of retroactive salary increases in one contract coupled with two years of prospective salary increases in another or, alternatively, a 1-year retro contract tied to a 3-year prospective contract. The problem with such arrangements is that they have been determined to be illegal, a concept the Acting Commissioner of Education established on Oct. 21, 2011, in *Board of Education of the Borough of Ramsey v. Ramsey Teachers Association* (Docket 48-2/11).

Relations between the Ramsey board and its union were so strained in June 2007 that it surprised no one when their contract expired without a new agreement. The board needed health insurance concessions and was willing to pay for them, but, deprived of bargaining tools such as *last best offer* by an NJEA-friendly legislature in 2003, it had only carrots in its "tool box," and no sticks. The union refused to budge, and impasse was declared. After state mediation failed, a PERC (Public Employment Relations Commission) fact-finder took over. By then, the process had turned ugly.

"Settle Now" signs and solidarity T-shirts appeared early, followed by more distressing job actions. Hand-scrawled posters attacking board members sprouted up. One board member received a nasty, anonymous letter at home. Board meetings became raucous, while union leaders ordered teachers not to write college recommendations, outraging parents and further dividing the town.

In this seething atmosphere, the fact-finder issued his report, which became public in February 2009. Although the recession was clearly underway, the fact-finder took no notice of it and recommended a three-year settlement, with 4.2 percent annual increases and no insurance concessions. He also suggested adding a fourth contract year, at 4.35 percent. Anxious to end the disharmony, the Ramsey board accepted the non-binding report. The union readily agreed, settling all issues and creating four years of salary guides that would extend through school year 2010-2011.

On April 28, 2009, two days before newly elected board members would be sworn in, the board approved the four-year deal, splitting it into two contracts: one with two years of retroactive salary increases, the other with two years of prospective increases.

State law (*N.J.S.A.* 18A:29-4.1) and a New Jersey Supreme Court decision, *Board of Education of the Township of Neptune v. Neptune Township Education Association, et al.*, 144 *N.J.* 16 (1996), prohibit a board from obligating itself or future boards for more than three years of teacher salary schedules. The statute reads, in pertinent part,

> A board of education of any district may adopt a one, two or three year salary policy, including salary schedules for all full-time teaching staff members . . . . Such policy and schedules shall be binding on the adopting board and upon all

future boards in the same district for a period of one, two, or three years from the effective date of such policy . . . .

In *Neptune*, the Court was considering whether that board, after a 3-year contract expired, was barred from paying increments during negotiations for a new contract. One reading of *Neptune* and *N.J.S.A.* 18 A:29-4,1 is that a board could not reach more than three years into the future with its salary schedules, leaving the door open to 2+2 or 1+3 contracts, thereby circumventing the law. But it is clear from the Court's opinion, the plain language of *N.J.S.A.* 18A:29-4.1, and legislative commentary that the determining factor is not length of contract, but the number of yearly salary schedules being implemented. The Neptune board's use of the old contract's third-year salary guide to pay increments in the year following expiration created a fourth year of salary policy, thereby violating the law.

One might argue that retroactive salary schedules do not violate the statute, but *N.J.S.A.* 18A:29-4.1 allows up to three years of salary policy "from the effective date of such policy." In *Newark Teachers Association v. Board of Education of Newark*, 108 *N.J. Super* 34 (L. 1969), affirmed 57 *N.J.* 100, the Court ruled that "effective date" did not mean date of adoption.

The effective date of the four yearly salary schedules adopted by the Ramsey board on April 29, 2009, was July 1, 2007, when the first one took effect, and the three-year limitation encompassed school years 2007-2008, 2008-2009, and 2009-2010. The salary schedule for 2010-2011, therefore, violated the prohibition against a fourth year. It didn't matter that the contracts were negotiated in good faith. As the Commissioner ruled in *Orlando v. Board of School Estimate*, OAL (Docket EDU 4550-83), "The salary schedules . . . while they may have been negotiated in good faith . . . fall outside the clear provisions of [Title 18A] and are of no effect."

The *Neptune* case also cited public policy reasons for the Court's decision.

> . . . the practice of automatically paying an increment will limit a board's ability to respond to ever-changing economic conditions . . . Schools that need to cut budget growth will face serious problems. Teachers will have reduced incentive to agree to a new [Agreement]. Indeed, teachers may resist negotiating and wait for more generous increments that will accrue . . . .

As school year 2011-2012 began, the Ramsey district found itself in a financial bind, unprecedented in its 103-year history. Its budgets had been defeated in 2008 and 2009, with approximately $1 million cut by municipal government. After Gov. Christie took office, $4 million in state aid was lost. Faced with that lost revenue, the two percent tax cap and union leaders who seemed likely to block any cost-saving measures, I wrote a legal brief supporting the idea that the 2+2 settlement was an illegal act that had to be rescinded and persuaded the board to have the matter reviewed by counsel.

The board attorney concurred with the analysis. Shortly thereafter, the board filed the action that led to the Acting Commissioner's Oct. 21, 2011, decision overruling an administrative law judge's earlier opinion and declaring the fourth year of Ramsey's 2+2 contracts "null and void." In doing so, the decision referred, with approval, to an unpublished appellate decision involving the Borough of Bogota that ruled the same way on similar facts.

An appeal to the decision has been filed by the Ramsey Teachers Association, but in light of this decision, school districts throughout the state should examine past practices to see if they, too, have inadvertently violated New Jersey law.

Chapter 35

School Leader published a second article of mine in its September-October 2012 edition, this one on a more expansive public policy issue, not only in New Jersey but throughout the nation.

Public Employee Unions: Are They in the Public Interest?

After Wisconsin Gov. Scott Walker ramrodded a bill through his legislature restricting collective bargaining rights of government employees, outraged unionists gathered a million signatures to force a June recall election. Walker trounced his opponent, dealing labor a bitter defeat.

Bias against the recall process aided Walker's cause, as did an overwhelming fund-raising advantage, but I believe recession-battered voters were also reacting against what they perceived as overly generous salaries and benefits for many public-sector workers.

Just days after Walker's victory, Indiana Gov. Mitch Daniels appeared on Fox News Sunday. Daniels, who had signed an executive order in 2005 eliminating union rights for state workers, explained his opposition to public-sector collective bargaining.

"There's a fundamental problem with government becoming its own special interest group," Daniels told Fox host Chris Wallace. "Forced dues [are] recycled into politics to elect compliant and friendly politicians in an unending circle," he said, "and ultimately there is not really bargaining in those situations because government sits on both sides of the table."

When Wallace asked the governor if he favored complete elimination of public employee unions, Daniels said, "I think government works better without them, I really do."

Unions like the New Jersey Education Association (NJEA) have long dominated politics in our own state—through their campaign contributions and, just as important, through their ability to mobilize members into a get-out-the-vote army on behalf of any chosen lawmaker . . . or against any targeted lawmaker.

Twelve percent of our labor force—560,000 workers—are employed by state and local government. Despite the political clout inherent in those numbers, New Jerseyans are decidedly behind the cost-cutting efforts of brash, *YouTube-ing* Gov. Chris Christie, who pointedly refused to seek NJEA's endorsement in his 2009 election bid.

NJEA represents 170,000 teachers, each paying $791 in dues. In 2011, the union doled out $486,000 in 87 separate contributions to legislative candidates—86 to Democrats and one to a Republican. It also donated $173,000 to Democratic Party committees and set aside $500,000 for school elections.

In pre-Christie days, NJEA played both sides, channeling one-third of its contributions to Republicans. I believe that the union now sees a larger number of beholden Democrats in the Legislature as its antidote to the governor.

This activity in the political arena—constitutionally protected and practically limitless, according to the Supreme Court's *Citizens United* decision, raises questions that might not have come up in better economic times. Are public employee unions in the public interest? In my opinion, the answer is an unequivocal *no*. Shrinking state aid, property tax caps, and ballooning health insurance costs have put school districts and municipalities in crisis mode. Not only do public employee unions drive up costs, they are patently inefficient. The collective bargaining process is a collective mess.

New Jersey has 585 school districts, 566 municipalities, 21 counties, and dozens of independent government agencies—each having multiple union locals negotiating separate contracts with widely disparate terms and conditions. For example, the Ramsey school district, where I serve as trustee, has four unions representing its employees; Ramsey Borough, where I once served as mayor, has six unions. Within those ten negotiated union contracts, there are no less than five different health insurance plans, some costing twice as much as others, and a veritable rat's nest of ancillary benefits.

There has to be a better way of determining fair compensation and benefits for public employees, and, recently, we saw what that better way might look like.

In June 2011 Gov. Christie signed a bi-partisan bill enacting pension and health benefits reforms for state and local workers—mandatory reforms that supersede any negotiated contract. The health benefits provisions, which take effect over four years, require all government workers to contribute toward the cost of their insurance, based on salary and coverage. An employee earning $50,000 and needing family coverage will contribute 12 percent of premium cost; employees making over $110,000 will pay the top contribution, 35 percent of premium.

Ramsey has a K-12 school district with 3,000 students and 440 full-time employees. What our district has been unable to achieve through negotiations, it now has gained through Christie's health benefits law. In school year 2012-2013, employees getting health insurance will contribute $1.1 million toward the cost. When the law is fully implemented in 2014, annual insurance contributions will approach $2.5 million.

Multiply Ramsey's experience by 585 school districts, and you can see how school taxes could eventually drop statewide by a billion dollars. Add employee contributions from 566 municipalities and 21 counties, and it is not hard to envision $2 billion in annual property tax relief—at no added cost to the state treasury and a reasonable cost-benefit ratio to employees.

New Jerseyans suffer the highest property taxes in the nation and rank among the highest taxed in almost every other category except gas taxes. Salaries and benefits are the largest component of municipal and school budgets and, hence, the biggest drivers of property taxes. The new pension and health benefits law is a *first* step in the right direction, but the question remains. Are public employee unions in the public interest? Our state legislature, sooner or later, must answer that question.

Part IV

The New Colossus of Trenton

Essays about *Jersey-Style* Politics and Governor Chris Christie

No, Governor Christie, this is *not* what we elected you to do!

New Jersey Schoolchildren Caught in the Crossfire

Democrats Cave to the New Colossus of Trenton

The "Not Me" State Budget

How the Democrats Should Have Played Their Hand

Christie Plays the Blame Game . . . Then Digs a Bigger Credibility Hole

New Governor, Same Old Hypocrisy

Something Missing From the Picture

A Tale of Two Christies

Rethinking Christie

Chapter 36

Although I supported many of Gov. Chris Christie's initiatives, particularly his resolve to control personnel costs in government, I was not a fan of his style of governing and frequently criticized some of his more onerous policies. My feelings about Christie became more positive (see Chapter 45, "Rethinking Christie," later in this book), but I have no hesitancy in presenting my still valid criticisms here. This piece is from "In the Arena," March 18, 2010.

No, Governor Christie, this is *not* what we elected you to do!

In his budget address to a joint session of the legislature on Tuesday, Governor Chris Christie disclosed his plans to rescue the State of New Jersey from its fiscal irresponsibility of the past. "The day of reckoning has arrived," he said, adding that the time had come to end the profligate ways of previous governors and legislatures. It is time, he said, to make the difficult decisions and hard choices necessary to right our ship of state.

I don't think any reasonable person could disagree with that sentiment; indeed, I was in the governor's corner right up until the time that I realized he didn't have the slightest clue as to what he was doing. Or, what havoc his proposed budget would wreak on local property taxpayers everywhere and on every suburban school district in the state.

Yes, bold action is required, but the governor would be wise to part with his "new-sheriff-in-town" attitude and start working with state legislators and seeking advice from political leaders who know what the challenges are at the local level—municipalities and school boards, alike.

The Democrat-controlled legislature got the message in the last election. They have already signaled to the governor they are prepared to work with him. The senate enacted significant pension system reforms, and the assembly was poised to do the same and send the bill to the governor's desk, until he beat up on them, too. This budget address was a slap in the face to bipartisanship, and we need bipartisanship to get through this crisis. The governorship in New Jersey might be the most powerful executive branch in the nation, but it is not a dictatorship.

The way the new governor has purposely picked a fight with the New Jersey Educational Association (NJEA), the statewide teachers' union, is disgraceful. I've seen schoolyard bullies display more grace and understanding. I am no NJEA apologist—I have written extensively on the over-the-top political influence of NJEA and its negotiating intransigence costing taxpayers millions. We can agree on that, but NJEA is clearly prepared to make a deal in this new political climate. It is apparent to any observer, except, perhaps, the governor, who tried to take the sharp edge off by saying rank-and-file teachers are just great—it's their union leaders he can't stomach.

All during this budget preparation process leading up to Tuesday's speech, the governor and Bret Schundler, Christie's new Education Commissioner, signaled to school districts that they could expect up to a 15 percent reduction in school aid in this upcoming fiscal year—July 1 to June 30th. While that figure is a steep decline in one year's time, all of us serving on school boards and working in school administration were prepared to live with it. We had already taken steps to factor that cut into our planning—planning that must take place on a very short time table to conform with the state's rules and regulations. School districts have to submit a preliminary budget to county superintendents by the morning of March 23rd to meet all the deadlines the state imposes in advance of the April 20th budget vote by citizens in each district.

Well, in his address, the governor revealed for the first time that he intends to cut state aid to education not by an average 15 percent, but by up to five percent of each district's total budget. Not five percent less school aid, but *all* school aid up to five percent of a district's total school budget.

In Ramsey, where I serve on the school board (after having served as mayor for four years), our school budget is about $47 million. Five percent of that is about $2.3 million. Ramsey's total state school aid is $2.191 million, and under Christie's planned budget, Ramsey has lost it all. In one fell swoop. In a time frame that gives us just six days to prepare for the worst financial catastrophe to hit our community in its 101-year existence.

This is not cutting the fat. Ramsey has one of the lowest ratios of administrators to students in the entire state. The only fault I find with the Ramsey school board's past management of its finances is something I have written about and have been taking steps to change. The Ramsey district did not make a good deal with its teachers in the last contract go-around. We gave them too much, and they were willing to concede too little. That is a past sin we are hell bent on correcting in the next contract negotiations. But that will take time and that will take some of the new "tools" the governor said he would be giving to municipalities and school boards to deal more effectively with recalcitrant public employee unions.

Without time to work these things out, Ramsey's public education system and public education in just about every other suburban school district—places where taxpayers willingly footed the bill to gain an enhanced education for their children—will suffer irreparable harm. Irreparable. This is not fat-cutting. It is muscle-cutting and sinew-cutting and bone-damaging.

I am not one of the special interests that Christie said would start railing against his budget and him, personally, because we don't want to endure the pain or make the hard choices. I am a volunteer who cares about his community and his community's children.

What could Christie have done differently? How could he have closed the budget gap without the drastic and draconian measures he has taken against public education? Well, for starters, he could have made the reductions in state aid more gradual, thereby giving school boards and administrators time to deal with the changes that will ensue. He could have given us that "tool kit" he talked about in his speech, so that we could negotiation new employee contracts fairer to property taxpayers.

Christie cut $819 million from state aid to education. If he had allowed the "millionaires tax" (the temporary tax, which expired in January, on New Jerseyans earning over $400,000 per year) to continue for a year or two, state aid to education could have been reduced more gradually.

The governor also could have done what courageous political leaders have recommended for years—allowed a 10-cent a gallon increase in the gasoline tax. New Jersey has the third or fourth lowest gasoline tax in the nation. In these days of wildly fluctuating gas prices, ranging upwards of $3.00 a gallon, who would notice a price of $3.10 instead of $3.00? No one. And this tax would also be paid by a lot of out-of-staters, who use our roads and bridges and pay nothing for their upkeep.

But no, the governor didn't take those reasonable steps because he uttered during his campaign the "read-my-lips" pledge of no new taxes. He was very short on particulars, you will remember, during his campaign. He refused to say how he would deal with our financial problems, except to make the crowd-pleasing promise to cut waste, fraud, and abuse. The ubiquitous promise of every politician who places electability ahead of truth.

It is time for state legislators to stand up to this governor's obstinate, know-it-all attitude, his ignorance of basic governance. It is time for former governors, some of whom still hold the respect of our citizens (Tom Kean and Brendan Byrne and Jim Florio, to name three) to speak out publicly on this issue. It is time for every citizen to tell this governor that we want him to solve the state's fiscal problems, but not do it on the backs of local property taxpayers. It is time for us to tell Chris Christie, "No, Governor, this is *not* what we elected you to do."

Chapter 37

I may have been a bit over the top in my attack on Christie in this Op-Ed piece from The Record on April 15, 2010, but my blood was up. The governor was urging voters to reject local school budgets if their teachers did not agree to his call for pay freezes. I was in favor of pay freezes, too, but I did not like the ham-handed approach of bringing down an entire school budget if freezes could not be achieved.

New Jersey Schoolchildren Caught in the Crossfire

The New Jersey Education Association (NJEA) and Gov. Chris Christie are going to the mattresses. So far, both sides have displayed all the finesse and restraint one might expect from a clash between headstrong Sonny Corleone and the Five Families.

As often happens in all-out war, neither combatant considers the unintended consequences of its actions. It is the immediate battle that matters, the need to inflict maximum casualties on one's opponent. Here's the problem: A lot of non-combatants will inevitably become "friendly-fire" casualties.

The governor has ignored what his budget proposal will do to New Jersey's school children, not just next fiscal year but long term. It is simply not on his radar screen. At a recent news conference, he urged voters in any district where teachers have rejected a wage freeze to vote down their school budget. Presently, that means he wants 577 out of 588 school districts to reject their budgets out of hand, with no regard for the details of those budgets or spending cuts and staff lay-offs already instituted or programs already slashed.

"The die is cast," said the governor's spokesperson. "This is the fight we've chosen and it's got to be had."

This is the first time in New Jersey history a governor has asked voters to turn their backs on public education, perhaps the most irresponsible act imaginable for the chief executive of a state. Christie's education aid cuts this fiscal year ($475 million) and his proposed cuts next fiscal year ($819 million) threaten to transform some of New Jersey's finest suburban school districts, turning them from models of excellence into models of mediocrity.

The NJEA is just as intractable: To give in to any part of the governor's program is unthinkable. NJEA is used to getting its way, thanks to millions it has contributed to legislative candidates over the years and an army of militant members it can put on the street or on the phones, for or against a candidate. In the pay-to-play world of Trenton politics, the 800-pound gorilla in the room expects to be heard. And compliant legislators have listened and obeyed, stacking the negotiating deck in favor of local teachers' unions and against property tax payers.

Christie's victory last November, despite the union's opposition, is the first chink in NJEA's electoral armor, and the union doesn't know how to handle it. Rather than reassessing the public's outrage over union obstinacy in a time of financial crisis, NJEA is conducting a straight-ahead assault on the governor, reminiscent of Pickett's charge at Gettysburg or the charge of the Light Brigade at Balaclava. Bold? Maybe. Smart? Not at all.

Discussion and compromise might have saved hundreds, if not thousands, of jobs for untenured teachers, the enthusiastic and idealistic ones just starting out. These young people and all those presently studying to become teachers, not to mention the many in high school contemplating such a career, may be lost to the profession forever.

For every thousand newly unemployed teachers, New Jersey will lose $60,000,000 in taxable state income, plus the collateral jobs and business activity such income creates in the private sector when it is spent. Laid-off teachers will continue to be a drain on school districts *and* taxpayers—about $15,000 a year per former employee, for unemployment insurance costs and the employer-funded portion of Cobra health insurance benefits. Some larger districts most hit by state aid cuts will see a $500,000 price tag for this new expense. In Ramsey, where I serve on the school board and where 15 full-time positions are being eliminated, we had to set aside $245,000 to cover unemployment insurance costs next year.

The NJEA's ubiquitous television ads feature photogenic teachers whose first concern is always the kids. Well, that idealized image of the profession will be put to rest. The union's refusal to budge in these tough economic times—not an inch, not even a millimeter—has turned the public against them, perhaps forever.

The governor will ultimately be exposed as the embodiment of the Peter Principle—someone who has risen to the level of his incompetence. His actions will cause property taxes to rise faster than they would have otherwise, while, at the same time, diminishing the quality of public education in New Jersey. We will be paying more and getting less for our money. As a result, he will be a one-term governor.

Christie was a failed freeholder, but an excellent fundraiser for George Bush. That got him the U.S. Attorney's post in New Jersey, where his my-way-or-the-highway persona fit in pretty well. The success of his staff's public corruption cases (I doubt if he, himself, has ever tried a criminal case) got him the governorship, an office not as well suited to bully-boy tactics.

In his former role as U.S. Attorney, Christie engineered plea bargains with the state's most corrupt politicians. You would think he'd be willing to negotiate a little on behalf of school children, young teachers, and local property taxpayers—the three groups hurt most by his actions. The victims of friendly fire.

Chapter 38

I took to calling Gov. Christie the "New Colossus of Trenton," a take, of course, on the Colossus of Rhodes, one of the seven wonders of the ancient world because of the way the 100-foot statue dominated the city of Rhodes. My applying this reference to the governor was not so much a comment on his physical size—something that has subjected him to being the butt of many jokes (no pun intended here)—as it was a comment on how he has so thoroughly dominated politics in New Jersey's capital. Here is an essay from "In the Arena" on June 6, 2010, that illustrates my point.

Democrats Cave to the New Colossus of Trenton

The schoolyard bully just stole the lunch money of Democrats in the state legislature, but don't shed any tears for that pitiful bunch. It was preordained they would cave to the governor over the state budget. He had the *cojones*, they did not.

The Record and *The Star-Ledger* both broke the news today about a reported budget deal between the Democratic controlled state legislature and Governor Christie. The Democrats are going to abdicate their co-equal branch responsibilities and allow passage of the Governor's $29.3 billion budget, getting in return a few disgraceful crumbs to assuage their shattered egos.

The governor's $819-million cut in state aid to education stays in the budget. Some school districts, like Ramsey where I live and serve on the school board, lost millions and were given less than a week to plan for that Freddy Kruger-like slashing of promised state aid. Those millions will be made up this next school year, in part, by suburban property taxpayers paying more in school taxes than they would have, otherwise, and by young, untenured teachers losing their jobs.

The governor's elimination of property tax rebates stays in the budget, too. He says he will replace rebates, maybe, with direct property tax credits sometime in the future, but don't hold your breath. The whole property tax rebate program was a politician-contrived gimmick to begin with.

Picture this. A con man comes to you and says, I am going to take $100 out of your left pocket, but don't worry, I will be putting $87 back in your right pocket. And I will return that "rebate" to you just before Christmas, so when you go out shopping, you will please think kindly of me for doing so. Laughable, right? Well, that is, in effect, the property tax rebate program. Just substitute Election Day for Christmas, and add a bunch of zeros to the numbers. Christie is right to do something about it. I don't object to his goal, just to his "end-justifies-the-means" way of getting there. Christie is still taking the $100 out of our left pocket. He just decided not to give us the $87 in our right pocket.

The higher income tax rate for those earning more than $1,000,000 a year (annual income, I said, not net worth) is gone. The Governor vetoed that measure, and Democrats are too timid to even bring it up again for an override attempt. True, their chances of getting a two-thirds vote to override are practically nil, but why not hold Republicans' feet to the fire and make them go on record as having more concern for the wealthy elite of this state than for the burdened middle class.

The New Jersey governor is, constitutionally, already the most powerful state chief executive in the nation. Given these latest actions of the Democratic controlled legislature, Gov. Christie might now be considered the only elected *dictator* in the nation, answerable to no one of consequence.

He can stack the New Jersey Supreme Court at will, as he recently proved. Don't think for a minute the Democratic controlled state senate, which is supposed to "advise and consent," will do anything about it. And, he now owns the state legislature. All three branches of government in New Jersey are now firmly under the control of one man, the new "decider."

Here's what Democrats got in this budget deal for turning over the keys of state government to Chris Christie. A few extra bucks for libraries, plus a hospital in Hunterdon County will stay open, plus Bergen County's blue laws will remain intact. That's all, folks. If that's the kind of negotiators Senate President Sweeney and Assembly Speaker Oliver are, we are in for big trouble these next three and a half years.

But wait, here is the best part. I saved it for last.

Democrats are going to let the Republicans write the budget bill (a task usually reserved for the majority party) and are going to supply four *yes* votes in the senate and eight in the assembly—just enough to pass the budget, assuming Republicans move in lock step with their Governor. Don't worry about the Democratic sacrificial lambs who will be picked to vote for the budget—they will come from the most gerrymandered and safest Democratic districts in the state.

Sweeney and Oliver and their pusillanimous partisans say they "don't like" the Governor's budget. By surrendering the bill-writing responsibility to Republicans and supplying the bare minimum votes necessary to pass it, the Democrats think they'll have plausible deniability.

Isn't that rich? They take a dive in the 14th round of the biggest budget battle in recent New Jersey history, and they are setting themselves up to pass the blame when middle class property taxpayers finally realize that Christie is not a cost-cutter—he is a cost-*shifter*, from state government to local property taxpayers.

Chapter 39

My continuing criticism of Trenton budget politics, from "In the Arena," on June 22, 2010.

The "Not Me" State Budget

When I used to read the "funny pages"—that's the name we old-timers called the comics section of our Sunday newspaper—there was one cartoon I liked a lot. It was cartoonist Bil (yes, one L) Keane's "The Family Circle" and it poked fun at the situations young parents experience in raising families. I think the syndicated feature is still around but now goes by the title, "The Family Circus."

Anyway, one recurring theme of the cartoon involved the three children getting into some minor mishap at home, like knocking over a vase or stepping on the cat's tail or bopping a sibling on the noggin with a toy. When the parent enters the room to ask who is responsible for the misdeed, each child shouts in unison, "Not me." The laugh arose when Bil Keane cleverly inserted a little gremlin running from the room, his ghostly attire inked with the name, "Not me."

This cartoon sprang to mind when I read the lead article in today's paper about the budget deal reached between the governor and the Democrat-controlled state legislature. It was already a foregone conclusion, as far as I was concerned, that the Democrats would grovel at the feet of the New Colossus in Trenton. The news story today just confirmed the height, or should I say depths, of their pusillanimity.

What really struck me today, though, was Governor Christie's crowing about the budget deal.

"We're going to wind up passing an historic budget that will close an $11 billion budget gap without tax increases," the governor said.

Of course, the governor is spewing forth pure bull manure—I'd use a more demonstrative word, but this is a PG-rated blog—and he is smart enough to know that. He is intentionally misleading the public by walking that very fine line lawyers learn early to walk: staying, just barely, on the *literally accurate* side of the line, while creating the false impression he wants to leave behind.

The governor's budget, swallowed whole by the Democrats with a handful of face-saving tidbits allowed by their master, will indeed raise taxes. Not income taxes. In fact, it cuts $1 billion in income taxes for the richest one or two percent of New Jersey residents. The Christie budget will raise every New Jerseyan's property taxes. Without a doubt. And when it happens, the governor will run from the room, with a "Not Me" smirk on his face.

When the governor ended the property tax rebate program ($848 million), cut state aid to public schools ($819 million), and reduced state aid to municipalities ($400+ million), who do you think will make up the difference? Yes, lots of public employees will be laid off, and that will make up part of those cuts. And lots of textbooks will not be bought and potholes will not be filled and sidewalks will not be repaired and extracurricular activities will not be offered and roads will not be patrolled. Yes, towns and school districts can make up part of those massive cuts by reducing expenses, eliminating services, and managing their personnel functions better—keeping in mind that at some point in the future, those chickens will come home to roost. Almost all the essential things not done today will have to be done, someday.

Dear friends and fellow citizens, you, in the end, will be making up the lion's share of those massive state cuts by paying increased property taxes in the coming year and by suffering massive service cuts and deteriorating schools and infrastructure in future years. Many school districts and towns in Bergen County lost millions in state aid in an instant, with no time to plan for the shortfall or renegotiate union contracts set in stone by existing state law. How can they cope with such draconian cuts without, in part, raising the tax levy on homeowners? It can't be done, not in the time frame the governor allowed us.

The governor and legislature are working on another deal, whereby property taxes will be capped in the future. The governor proposes a 2.5 percent "hard" cap (no exceptions), which would be embedded in our state constitution; the Democrats in the legislature propose a 2.9 percent "soft" cap (some exceptions) through legislation, not a constitutional amendment. I happen to like the governor's plan better, with a few modifications, and have no doubt he will prevail once again over this legislature. But we need his promised tool kit to bring personnel costs, which make up 60-75 percent of most local budgets, under better control. So far, we haven't got it.

I've said before that I support the overall goal of bringing local personnel costs under better control . . . and I said it long ago, when Chris Christie was just settling into his U.S. Attorney's position, his reward for raising so much campaign money for George W. Bush. What I don't support is this governor's methods, his short-sightedness, and his duplicity in accomplishing that goal. Let me give you one example—this one on short-sightedness.

Christie cut $7.5 million from a program that provided 65,000 free Pap tests and 75,000 free breast examinations last year for poor women in New Jersey. Early detection of cervical and breast cancer is crucial to survival rates for those diseases, right? I don't think anyone would dispute that. Most of those women, I would assume, are in the lower income brackets and without health insurance. Many will forego these tests because they can't afford them.

And what is the logical result? More will get advanced stages of those diseases before they are detected, cutting down on their survival rates and costing many more millions in indigent health care that New Jersey citizens will pay for eventually.

Do you see my point? Let's say this program improves the early detection rate in just one percent of those examined. That means hundreds of women will learn about their cancer much sooner, when it is more treatable. Many will live longer lives as a result, but we will all benefit because millions of dollars—far more than the $7.5 million annual cut Christie made—will not have to be spent treating the advanced stages of these diseases.

I haven't examined the budget closely, but I'd bet there are dozens of such examples. Eventually, the public will see through the Christie façade. I hope it comes soon enough to prevent a second term and what surely will be the further demise of our state.

P.S. I stopped reading the funny pages when the news section provided me with all the laughs I needed.

Chapter 40

My unheeded advice to Democratic legislators, from "In the Arena," June 23, 2010.

How the Democrats Should Have Played Their Hand

Some Democratic legislators have suggested they just *had* to give in to Governor Christie's draconian state budget because the alternative was too upsetting—a shutdown of state government come July 1st, when the new fiscal year starts. Under New Jersey law, if the new fiscal year's budget is not passed, the state cannot expend funds. Because the governor would not accept any significant changes to his proposed budget (yes, he threw the Dems a few crumbs) and was apparently willing to let the state go to Hell in order to get his way, Democratic leaders (if you can call them that) folded and the governor scooped the pot. He'd make a great No Limit Texas Hold'em player, he would.

Here's how those weak-kneed, shoulder-quaking, lip-quivering Democrats in the state legislature should have played their hand.

Senate President Sweeney and Assembly Speaker Oliver should have called a press conference and made the following joint statement:

> *We wish to advise Governor Christie and our Republican colleagues that their proposed budget is unacceptable to the Democratic majorities in both houses of our state legislature. We have been willing to work with the governor these past few months to find common ground and a workable path to future financial health for New Jersey, but the governor has insisted that he get his way on every issue of significance. We remind the governor that this state is not a dictatorship and that our state constitution mandates that the separate branches work together to govern our state. The governor has brandished the bludgeon of a state government shutdown if he does not get his way on every important issue. Well, if that is his attitude, then let the shutdown begin.*

But before we depart, here are a few things for the governor to consider. We make these proposals as a package, and not for the governor to cherry-pick and accept just the things that go his way and reject the things he doesn't like. This is presented as a compromise, which is how the Founding Fathers of this great nation and this state expected government to operate.

1. We are willing to vote tomorrow to put on the state ballot this November a 2.5 percent hard cap on future property tax levy increases, as the governor has proposed, with two minor modifications. First, voters will be able to approve increases greater than 2.5 percent by a simple majority vote, not the 60 percent super-majority the governor has proposed. If a majority of voters give their approval, there is no logical reason to stand in the way of the will of the people. Second, this new amendment, if it is approved by voters, will take effect in two years. Municipalities and school districts must be given time to adjust to these changes by negotiating more fiscally prudent employee contracts and finding other ways to economize. It would be irresponsible to require local governments to make this significant change in a shorter time frame. In the meantime, they will have to live within the 4 percent cap already in place.

2. We are willing to pass legislation that will give the governor his 33-point tool kit to allow local governments and school districts to negotiate more effectively with their public employee unions. We want to further fine tune that package of proposals and will work with the governor to come up with an acceptable final form of legislation, but we are committed in principle to move forward with his initiative in this regard.

3. We will move forward to advise and consent on his recent appointment to the New Jersey Supreme Court and will continue to do so with all his future appointments. While we deplore his politicization of the independent judiciary this state has prided itself on, we recognize the governor has the authority to do what he did and not reappoint an outstanding jurist, simply to remake the Court in his own image. So be it. We will let the people decide in the next gubernatorial election if that is the way they want their state to operate.

4. We will accept the governor's proposed state budget in its entirety, with the following exception. The so-called millionaire's income tax surcharge will be restored to the way it was during the last fiscal year—that is, an added tax on annual incomes of more than $400,000—and will be allowed to remain in place for three additional years to give this state time to find alternative revenue sources and to cut additional expenses. During that time frame, the annual revenue raised by this tax surcharge, approximately $1 billion, will be used to restore one-half of the state aid to education that the governor originally cut and one-half of the property tax rebate program the governor originally cut. This will give school districts time to make the transition to leaner operating budgets and will give the state time to replace property tax rebates with a direct property tax credit for those low-income seniors and disabled citizens who need assistance. Both the school aid restoration and the property tax rebate restoration will translate into property tax relief for strapped New Jersey homeowners. The balance of the revenue generated from the tax surcharge will be used to restore vital programs the governor has cut, like cervical and breast cancer screenings for indigent women, care for the mentally ill, and other programs this legislature deems necessary. We will work with the governor to try to come up with restorations acceptable to both sides.

If the governor is unwilling to compromise to this very slight degree—getting perhaps 95 percent of what he wanted, but giving up just a little to make the necessary transition less onerous for property taxpayers and less painful to those who find it hardest to endure that pain—then, we are prepared to wait him out for as long as it takes. With that in mind, we have passed legislation to encourage state workers to stay on the job, without pay, until a new budget is passed, with the promise they will be reimbursed retroactively for the days they have worked without pay. This legislation also promises vendors they will be paid for goods and services supplied during the shutdown, once the new budget is enacted. Those bills are on the governor's desk and will ease the crisis if he persists in his unwillingness to compromise. He can veto them, if it is his desire to make this crisis even larger than it already is. Or he can sign them with the hope that essential state services can continue until the crisis is resolved. It is his choice now. The ball is in his court, and the entire state is now focused on his qualities as a leader. Will he insist on a 100 percent victory and choose chaos, or will he accept a 95 percent victory and choose compromise.

We need better poker players in the New Jersey state legislature.

Chapter 41

Gov. Christie's actions regarding the state's "Race to the Top" application for federal education funds, and his tossing aside of Education Commissioner Bret Schundler when things went wrong, produced a low point in my respect for him. These next two related essays are from "In the Arena," on August 25 and August 27, 2010, respectively.

Christie Plays the Blame Game . . .

By now, you've heard about New Jersey losing out on a $400,000,000 "Race to the Top" (RTTT) federal grant to public education because some bureaucrat in the Christie administration filled out one of the application pages incorrectly. The governor held a news conference today, in which he accepted "responsibility" for the mistake.

It was an insincere gesture on his part. In almost the same breath as his *stand-up-guy* posturing, Christie showed what a sham his public persona really is. He blamed the Obama administration for New Jersey's defective grant application. No one in the administration called him, you see, to tell him the application was defective. As if that is all they have to do right now. The rules of the competition were clear. Once filed, the application had to stand. No amendments were permitted. Christie, as U.S. Attorney, prosecuted people all the time for not adhering to the rules. I don't recall him giving many people a second chance.

How did this fiasco happen? Sure, someone didn't read the instructions carefully and entered figures for fiscal years 2010 and 2011, instead of fiscal years 2008 and 2009, as required. Human error. But here, the context in which that error occurred is the significant point. And after a close examination of that context, we see that Christie is, indeed, the responsible party. I mean, really responsible—not just *play-acting* responsible.

State Education Commissioner Bret Schundler, Christie's appointment, spent days hammering out a compromise with the New Jersey Education Association, the statewide teachers' union Christie has been battling since before he took office. That compromise was important, because gaining the support of teachers would have enhanced New Jersey's chances for success in the RTTT competition. It would also have gained us extra points, so that our award may even have exceeded the 10th place amount of $400,000,000, which went to Ohio. New Jersey, in 11th place, got nothing.

Ohio beat us out by less than 5 points, and that margin was completely attributable to this one error. Without the error, we would have scored higher than Ohio and would have finished 10th. But if the application had had the support of the NJEA, which Schundler achieved, it is almost certain we would not only have surpassed Ohio, but probably other states as well, gaining for New Jersey's school kids hundreds of millions more in federal funds.

Christie threw out Schundler's compromise and scrapped the entire application the Commissioner's staff had completed. This last minute trashing of his own appointee's reputation and prestige to make a few cheap political points for himself was the ultimate cause of New Jersey's embarrassing failure in the RTTT competition. (We were the laughing stock, once again, of every evening news program tonight.) The Department of Education had to re-do the RTTT application in a matter of hours, because of Christie's petulant insistence on having it all his way. And in that kind of atmosphere—a hurried scramble to complete a complicated task—mistakes often happen, as they did here.

No, it wasn't the fault of the mid-level state employee who misread an instruction. It was the fault of the New Colossus of Trenton, who has misread his election victory last November as a license to dictate, not govern.

* * *

. . . Then Digs a Bigger Credibility Hole

One of last Sunday's newspapers carried a feature story about Governor Chris Christie's years as a student, including comments by some of his former teachers. It was instructive, but I think it missed an important aspect of young Chris's school days. Schoolboy Chris Christie, if his current skills are any indication, had to have been an outstanding dodge-ball player.

You've heard of the "non-apology apology" we often get from politicians caught in any wrong-doing? You know what I mean. It is the "mistakes were made" comment, or "I apologize if my remarks were taken wrong by anyone" comment. The elected official gives the appearance of apologizing, but actually says nothing about his own culpability for the action.

Gov. Christie has taken that political tactic in a new direction. He has perfected the *"non-acceptance of responsibility—responsibility acceptance"* maneuver. Here is how it works.

You start off by saying that you are in charge, so the responsibility is yours. Sort of like "The Buck Stops Here" sign on President Harry Truman's desk, except that Harry Truman was the real deal—I should be ashamed of myself for even mentioning him in the same paragraph as the New Colossus of Trenton.

Then, you pull a "Christie" and start pointing fingers at anyone— anyone at all—it doesn't matter if there is any foundation to the accusation or not.

Last Tuesday, after it became known that New Jersey lost out on $400 million in federal aid to education because of an incorrect application, Christie called it a "clerical" error and blamed the Obama administration for not allowing State Education Commissioner Bret Schundler or his staff to correct the error at a application review meeting they had in Washington, D.C., with the judges for the Race to the Top competition.

The U.S. Department of Education released a video today that showed Schundler and his staff being given every opportunity during that meeting to make the correction. They were asked repeatedly if they had the correct information, and repeatedly they said they could not come up with the figures. They didn't make any phones calls to get the correct information; they didn't go to the state web site to get the correct information. (Those were the two actions Christie faulted President Obama for not taking.) The New Jersey officials just sat there like dummies, hemming and hawing, and not having a clue what to do.

When confronted with this evidence of his misstatements on Tuesday, Christie said he was only repeating what he was told by his staff. Well, I guess it is pretty clear that his staff lied to him about what occurred at that meeting with federal officials. The point is this—what are you going to do about it now, Governor Christie? Are you going to apologize for your attack on the Obama administration for being too rigid in its technical approach to education—the charges you levied last Tuesday? Are you going to admit, for once, that you were wrong about something? Furthermore, are you going to hold those in your administration who allegedly lied to you accountable? If you don't, I think there will be a strong suspicion that no one lied to you, that you, yourself, were the dissembler-in-chief.

And here's a question for the Democratic leadership of the state legislature. What are *you* going to do about this $400 million loss of federal grant money for New Jersey's public education kids? After you acquiesced to more than a billion in state aid cuts to education in this new budget with barely a whimper, what are you going to do to get to the bottom of this fiasco? Here is my bet on that. Given your past history of political cowardice, my money is on the big Zip. Nothing. You may make some noise, but you will do nothing of substance about the Christie administration's mishandling of this entire episode.

Chapter 42

The political hypocrisy shown by most elected leaders gives me and other writers a target-rich environment in public policy matters. Gov. Christie crucified former governors and legislatures for excessive state debt and continued borrowing, but then embraced the idea of more borrowing for transportation infrastructure, instead of biting the bullet and advocating for the more fiscally prudent option of a modest gasoline tax increase. Here's my "In the Arena" blog post of October 5, 2010.

New Governor, Same Old Hypocrisy

The New Colossus of Trenton was true to his word. The governor said that unless the state legislature approved his plan of new borrowing and new debt restructuring (that means kicking the can down the road so that future governors have to worry about the fiscal consequences), he would call a precipitous halt to all on-going road construction projects in the state. And that is just what he did on Monday, October 4th.

The jobs were halted, workers went home on a taxpayer-paid holiday, and construction ceased. It didn't take long for the Democratic state legislature to once again cave to the pressure. They made a "deal" with the governor's Transportation head on the same day as the shutdown. They would approve the new debt if the governor would "try" to have an overall plan for the future financial soundness of our state's Transportation Trust Fund by December.

How pathetic this whole cast of characters makes our state look, from a state legislature that follows the *Chicken Little* school of crisis management, with courage to match, to a governor who, it is becoming increasingly apparent, intends to jump to the national stage in 2012, before the mess he has created in New Jersey through his arrogance and ineptitude metastasizes. (Send us a postcard from Iowa, Governor.)

The Transportation Trust Fund was created in the 1980s to provide a self-funding pool of resources to build and repair New Jersey's roads, bridges and other infrastructure. It also provides a subsidy for mass transit, the theory being that encouragement of greater mass transit use helps keep down the wear and tear on our roads and saves energy. The Trust Fund was supposed to get its resources from a variety of dedicated taxes, chief among which is the motor fuels tax, commonly known as the "gas tax."

As time went on, costs to build the projects and make the repairs grew, but the funding sources did not grow accordingly. The Trust Fund began to have shortfalls, but instead of adjusting the taxes to keep up with the need, governors from both parties and their complicit state legislatures took the easy way out—they simply borrowed money against future revenues to keep up with the needs. Debt grew from under $100 million in the early 1990s to more than $800 million today, while the gas tax, the chief source of funding, stayed the same—about 10.5 cents per gallon of gas. New Jersey has the fourth lowest gas tax in the country.

Where would the harm have been, in this new marketplace of $3 to $4 per gallon gas prices, to increase that gas tax by a dime per gallon? It would have hardly been noticeable to most drivers, but would have eventually lifted us out of this huge financial mess the Trust Fund now owns. A mess that is sure to get worse because of the new borrowing this governor rammed through the legislature in his typical bully-boy fashion, with absolutely no long-term planning for the future. Borrowing, the governor said, was part of the evil he inherited (true), but he now perpetuates that evil because it is convenient for him to do so. For all his tough talk, this governor now shows his true stripes. He is part of the same old hypocrisy and same old failure of leadership.

The NJ Transportation Trust Fund will be bankrupt in mid-2011, according to most experts. Look for another round of borrowing next year—anything to get Chris Christie to the 2012 finish line. He may be gone after 2012, but we New Jerseyans will be left holding the feed bag . . . and cleaning up the manure.

Chapter 43

The governor is going to hate this book, if he ever reads it. Chapter 45 might be the one exception. Here is a little fun, from "In the Arena," on October 25, 2010.

Something Missing From the Picture

It was the custom in ancient Rome to award a triumphal procession to a conquering general. Scipio Africanus got one when he kicked Carthage's butt. Hadrian got one when he walled up the troublemaking Brits in the North to keep them away from the peace-loving, tax-paying Brits to the South. All Rome turned out to hail the returning hero. Animals were sacrificed to his glory; maidens tossed flowers in his path.

The general rode in the finest chariot, no doubt upholstered in rich, Corinthian leather and pulled by a magnificent team of stallions. He was alone in the chariot, except for one servant, who stood immediately to his master's rear and who, throughout the tumultuous procession, whispered in the general's ear the same reminder, over and over: "All fame is fleeting. All fame is fleeting. All fame is fleeting."

Governor Chris Christie, the New Colossus of Trenton, has been on his own kind of triumphal procession for the past few months, appearing at partisan gatherings throughout the country to lend his fame to any Republican candidate in need of a boost. Things were going so well for us taxpayers here at home that the Governor was able to slip away to California, New Mexico, Ohio, Illinois, Pennsylvania, Massachusetts, and Iowa—collecting IOU's from the Republican faithful, while denying his own ambition for higher office.

Remember that tool kit he promised—the set of laws that would enable municipalities and school districts to negotiate more effectively with public employees unions so as to hold down personnel costs, three-quarters of every local budget? He pushed through the two percent cap on property taxes, but promised the tool kit so towns and schools could live within the cap and not disrupt vital municipal services and our schools.

Well, the tool kit is stalled in the state legislature, as public employee unions gain strength from Christie's absences and his recent string of missteps, like killing the ARC tunnel, its thousands of good construction jobs, and New Jersey's chance at a sound economic future. Like his ego-driven botching of a $400 million federal grant to public education—the same public education system he has trashed by reducing its state-funding by more than a billion dollars.

Christie's popularity is still high, but soon people will realize the spending cuts he made were mostly cuts in property tax relief programs. Even with those cuts, we are on the road to financial ruin, and he makes none of the really hard choices to get us off that road.

In most of the campaign photos we see, Governor Christie, always in shirtsleeves to show his connection to us common folk, has his arms outstretched in triumph. The Republican candidate he is pushing in California, Ohio, or wherever, is there next to him, but something is missing from the picture. I haven't noticed anyone standing behind Christie, whispering in his ear.

Chapter 44

Here is another swipe at political hypocrisy, courtesy of a U.S. Justice Department report issued in late 2010. This essay is from The Record on December 1, 2010.

A Tale of Two Christies[19]

A set of rules for Christie, a set for the rest of us

It was "the best of times" back then for U.S. Attorney for New Jersey Chris Christie, with a Republican in the White House and a bumper crop of Democratic malfeasants at hand in his home state. Christie had helped George W. Bush become president by being his chief fundraiser in New Jersey, and Bush rewarded his Jersey money man with a plum. Despite Christie never having tried a criminal case in court, Bush made him chief law enforcement officer for New Jersey, saving the failed one-term Morris County Freeholder from obscurity.

Christie did a good job at his new post. He was an able front man for a first-rate prosecutor's office that racked up conviction after conviction, mostly of corrupt public officials. You break the rules, you go to jail—no *ifs*, *ands*, or *buts*. Christie's pugnacious persona would brook no deviation from those rules. You were either with the good guys or with the bad guys. Step over the line a little, and WHAM! He got you.

You had to conform to Christie's strict code of ethics. Everyone did. Unless . . .well, unless you were Christie.

The United States Justice Department recently released information that five U.S. Attorneys had failed to abide by the department's rules regarding travel expenses, overcharging taxpayers thousands of dollars for their work-related trips. Among the five was our very own Chris Christie.

Christie's transgressions didn't amount to a lot of money—less than $3,000, it seems. That's not the point. The point is that his flouting of travel expense restrictions shows the man's arrogance, his willingness to live by two sets of rules—one for himself and one for everyone else. It is a trait that has carried over to his new job.

The Justice Department report said of the five transgressors (50 other U.S. Attorneys lived within the travel expense parameters) that they "exhibited a noteworthy pattern of exceeding the government rate and whose travel documentation provided insufficient, inaccurate or no justification for the higher lodging rates." Christie exceeded the approved rate for hotels in 14 of his 23 expense-paid trips during six years in office— about four boondoggles a year—without providing proper documentation for the over-billing. In some cases, he paid more than twice the acceptable lodging rate. When pressed for an explanation, Christie said, through a spokesperson, he couldn't find "decent" lodging near his convention site at the approved rate.

I suppose someone who believes himself entitled to *five-star* accommodations at taxpayer expense would be put out by a hotel that didn't provide fluffy bathrobes for its guests or a Godiva chocolate on the pillow at night. But Christie's extravagance on public-financed excursions didn't stop at his lodging preferences. After one trip to Boston, he ordered a limo to make the four-mile journey from his hotel to Logan Airport. What would a four-mile taxi ride cost? $25, with tip? $35? Christie billed taxpayers $236 for his limo to the airport.

On another "work-related" trip to London at taxpayer expense, he billed us for a $562 limousine ride. (Yes, I said London, England. Would someone please explain why we had to send the U.S. Attorney to a conference in Europe?)

Like I said—two sets of rules. One set for Christie, who was still traipsing around the country up to Election Day, appearing in a dozen states on behalf of Republican candidates and, perhaps, on behalf of Chris Christie. A recent guest on NBC's "Meet the Press," he denied being interested in running for president, at least in 2012; he left the door open for 2016, though—wide open.

I'm sure Republican campaign contributors paid most of the expenses for Christie's frequent pre-election jaunts, thereby allowing him the best of hotels, first-class air travel, and door-to-door limousine service without need for pesky accountability. Even so, we New Jersey taxpayers picked up the tab for his security detail *and* for the mischief-making of Democratic state legislators during his absence. Christie's much-touted "tool kit" may, indeed, make it through the legislature, but likely as a watered down version that may hardly be worth the effort. If the governor had paid attention to our business instead of the business of the national

Republican Campaign Committee during most of the summer and fall, perhaps the result would have been different.

And, it seems, there is another set of rules for New Jersey taxpayers, who must endure many more years of severe cutbacks and three more years of Governor Christie shifting the state's financial woes to local property taxpayers, without giving us the means to shoulder that burden. His *new rules*.

Governor Christie appeared recently before *The Record's* Editorial Board to answer questions about his first ten months in office. He claimed to be having "a lot of fun" being governor. It is going to be the worst of times for New Jersey for a long, long time, I'm afraid, even as Chris Christie's best of times continues.

Chapter 45

And then comes this final essay, on how I became a born-again Christie fan, thanks to the governor's unflagging political courage—the trait I admire most in any politician, even those whose opinions and policies I may differ with. This was a Sunday Opinion section feature in The Record on December 2, 2012.

Rethinking Christie[20]

I've been a frequent Christie critic, but the guy is beginning to grow on me. I'll admit that it took a while to get past his abrasive manner. When they doled out *attitude* to us Jersey natives, Chris Christie was first in line.

I blasted the governor early on, for urging voters to defeat local school budgets if teachers refused a pay freeze. ("N.J. schoolchildren caught in the crossfire," *The Record*, April 15, 2010.) With little notice, he slashed state aid to suburban school districts and turned students into friendly-fire victims in his war with the teachers' union.

"In his former role as U.S. Attorney," I wrote, "Christie engineered plea bargains with the state's most corrupt politicians. You would think he'd be willing to negotiate a little on behalf of schoolchildren, young teachers, and property taxpayers—three groups hurt most by his actions."

Eight months later, after the Justice Department released details on five U.S. Attorneys, Christie among them, who violated expense account regulations, I let loose with another Op-Ed broadside. ("A set of rules for Christie, a set for the rest of us," *The Record*, December 1, 2010.) Christie was preaching a *Mack-the knife* approach to fiscal solvency, but had opted for high-end hotels and expensive limo service while on taxpayer-funded jaunts as U.S. Attorney.

But just as political hypocrisy can provoke me into a writing frenzy, so too can political courage cause me to swoon. And it is becoming increasingly apparent that Gov. Chris Christie has political courage in abundance.

---

[20] © 2012 The Record (Bergen Co., NJ) / NJMG. Reprinted with permission.

The Sohail Mohammed affair is a case in point. Last year, Christie nominated the Muslim-American lawyer for a judgeship, bringing on a torrent of criticism, mostly from Republicans. It took courage to nominate Mohammed, especially while some conservative commentators were doing all they could to stir up anti-Muslim fears and prejudices. Christie's zealous and eloquent defense of his judicial nominee went beyond courage. It may well have been the defining political moment of this young century.

At a press conference, a reporter asked the governor what was behind the intense criticism of his appointment of Sohail Mohammed.

"Ignorance," was Christie's reply. Calling Mohammed an "outstanding American" who just happens to be Muslim, Christie went into full-blown, *Jersey-boy* mode.

"This Sharia law business is crap," Christie said. "It's just crazy, and I'm tired of dealing with the crazies. It's just unnecessary to be accusing this guy of things just because of his religious background."

Swoon. As a constitutional law professor, how could I help myself? When was the last time you heard Article VI, Clause 3 of our Constitution, banning religious tests for public office, put into practice by a politician?

This streak of independence appealed to me, but I was also becoming increasingly impressed by Christie's governing ability. In June 2011, Christie pushed through the Democrat-controlled, union-friendly state legislature a bill to reform pension and health benefits for public employees, a move that will save municipalities and school districts more than a billion a year once the law is fully implemented in 2014. It is the greatest property tax relief program in state history, and it didn't cost the treasury one dime. The savings come from requiring public employees to pay a reasonable share—less than one-third, in most cases—of their health insurance premiums, instead of foisting the entire cost on taxpayers.

What are we to make of our Jekyll and Hyde governor? Is the hard edge he often displays an essential component of leadership? In "Lincoln," the new Spielberg movie, we see the man revered as our greatest president acting, at times, like an overbearing, cajoling, wheeling and dealing, archetypal politician, willing to do almost anything to achieve his public policy objective.

I'm not comparing Christie to Lincoln, but what I am saying is that success "in the arena," as Teddy Roosevelt noted in his famous speech at the Sorbonne, sometimes requires our political leaders to be "marred by dust and sweat and blood." Roosevelt didn't say whose blood.

I had to learn more about this man and decided to attend one of the governor's "town hall" meetings—his never-ending road trip since taking office. On a beautiful, early summer day, I lined up at the entrance to Ramapo Ridge School in Mahwah, awaiting my chance to see and hear Chris Christie in person. I'd seen clips of his put-downs at these events, but, on this particular occasion, there were no fireworks—likely a disappointment for the media. Christie was polite to everyone who spoke. It was the most adept political performance I think I've ever witnessed. The governor has an imposing presence in any setting, but his command over the audience that day was astonishing. I went away almost a true-believer.

Then came Sandy.

I'm not alone in giving the governor high marks, not only for managing this disaster well, but also for displaying, once again, courage and independence. According to a Quinnipiac University poll published this past Tuesday, 95 percent of the polling sample rated Christie's handling of the storm's aftermath as excellent or good, and 72 percent approved of his overall job performance—the highest approval rating ever recorded by the Quinnipiac poll for a New Jersey governor. A day earlier, Fairleigh Dickinson University's *PublicMind* poll measured Christie's approval rating at an astounding 77 percent.

When Christie praised President Obama and the federal government's response to Sandy, just days before the election, it was as though he had committed sacrilege. Desperate for a scapegoat to explain losing an election they expected to win, Republicans, especially those who consider him too moderate to be the Party's 2016 standard bearer, were quick to blame Christie for Mitt Romney's demise.

Chris Christie's presidential ambitions are no secret. I don't know if his transgressions against Republican orthodoxy will hurt. The "crazies," after all, control that process. And there's still his re-election hurdle in *blue-state* New Jersey, come November 2013. Christie made it official this past Monday and announced his intention to run for a second term, bolstered in part by his high approval ratings, among Democrats and Independents as well as Republicans.

I'm not sure how I'll vote if Chris Christie makes it to the national stage, where the stakes are higher. Engaging world leaders, preferably in diplomacy but in war if necessary, is a lot different from taking on the president of the New Jersey Education Association. *Putin put-down* is not the page-one headline I'd want to read in a newspaper tabloid.

But I now know where my inclination lies at the state level, despite earlier misgivings. If kids had been operating a Kool-Aid stand outside Ramapo Ridge School when I left the town hall meeting on that hot day last June, I'd have ordered up the large-sized cup.

ACKNOWLEDGMENTS

I've enjoyed an 11-year relationship with *The Record* of Bergen County, as a freelance contributor, and with that newspaper's parent company, North Jersey Media Group (NJMG), as a columnist for one of its community newspapers and a citizen blogger on its website. Indeed, most of the essays in this book first appeared as Op-Ed pieces in *The Record* or as blog posts on NorthJersey.com. I must express my sincere appreciation to Peter Grad, who is my Op-Ed page editor at *The Record* and who has provided me with an abundance of writing assignments and has allowed me great latitude in expressing my often controversial views on public policy issues that matter to me. Also, I'm grateful for the many kindnesses shown to me by Malcolm Borg, NJMG Chairman, and by Stephen Borg, NJMG President and Publisher of *The Record*. Amre Youssef, NJMG Director of Content Syndications and Archives, was especially helpful to me in arranging permissions and being my primary contact at NJMG.

The photo insert is a meaningful part of this book, for me and my friends and family. I hope, too, that it touches every reader with a sense of what family means for most second-generation Americans, no matter what country their parents and forebears emigrated from. I am indebted to my cousin Vincent Muti and my sister Rita Bowerfind for combing their family albums and supplying me with many of the photos I used.

Tom Dater, Ramsey's Borough Historian as well as a dear friend (and, in my mind, the First Citizen of Ramsey), supplied me the political photos of my father. Tom's family goes back farther in Ramsey's history than probably any other. In addition to being prominent citizens of our town for more than 150 years, they owned and operated our local weekly newspaper, *The Ramsey Journal*. As a kid, I sold copies of that paper every Thursday, earning a nickel for each copy—half the selling price. I also want to thank Celeste Ranck, who works for Tom and his son, Chris Dater, for her help in producing for me good quality digital images of photos from the Dater Archives.

Bobby Major, a photography expert at The Photo Place in Ramsey, has been extremely helpful to me, not only in converting most of the family photos in this book to electronic versions, but also in doing the same for my prior book, *The Charmer*. Jeff Herbert, of Herbert Studios in Delaware, provided me with the author's photo on the back cover. Jeff, when he lived in Ramsey, was my father's neighbor and friend.

New York Times bestselling author Linda Fairstein took time from her hectic schedule to read a draft of this book and provide me with a most welcome blurb, as did my colleague at Fairleigh Dickinson University, Dr. Peter Woolley, who is a professor of comparative politics at that university's Florham Park campus. David Klass, a prolific and talented screenwriter, and Paul Dinas, one of publishing's most respected editors, both took an interest in my writing and both provided encouragement, as well as much appreciated blurbs. Dr. Larry J. Sabato, Director of the University of Virginia's Center for Politics and a frequent television commentator on the American political scene, also reviewed my draft of *Essays for my Father* and wrote a blurb—no small gesture for a man as busy as he.

Erika Block is responsible for the striking cover of this book and its interior design. I am very appreciative of her highly professional efforts on my behalf, performing the same top-notch work as she did for my previous book, *The Charmer*.

Finally, I would be a sad character, indeed, if I didn't acknowledge my wife, Lorraine, for her steadfast support and encouraging words, as I put together this very personal and emotional project.

OTHER BOOKS BY RICHARD MUTI

NON-FICTION

The Charmer:
The True Story of Robert Reldan—Rapist, Murderer, and
Millionaire—and the Women who Fell Victim to his Allure
(print and eBook editions)

Passion, Politics and Patriotism in Small-Town America:
Confessions of a plain-talking independent mayor
(print edition only)

FICTION

Good Lawyer, Dead Lawyer
A Novel
(print and eBook editions)

Available wherever books are sold.